The Time Mastery System has been life changing for me professionally. What might look like to some as a "to do" list is actually an effective plan for taking back control of your day. When you take back control, you are no longer bogged down by the tasks that take your valuable time away. You begin reaping the benefits on the first day, but its true results manifest themselves weeks down the road. I now have the time to focus on the "long-term" objectives, or the "improving myself" items that always seemed to get pushed off until tomorrow. Try it. Stay with it. Change your life!

JIM REARDON
Production Manager
RI Kitchen & Bath Inc.

I have been using Mark's Mastering Time for several months now. Not only does it help me whittle time from my day by staying on track, but it also helps me leave my day feeling more accomplished. I couldn't live without it now and would encourage anyone to give it try.

JENN HARBICK
The Neil Kelley Companies

Mark's system Mastering Time has been invaluable and has provided something that is almost impossible. It has provided me a format that has given me additional time during the day, allowing me to be more effective and efficient. Thanks Mark, for both the inspiration and guidance.

BEN LAMON
Director of Sales Closet America

Probably the most important time-management training seminar I have ever attended. I took this seminar early in my career and have used it throughout my professional life in a variety of roles. Mark's system is easy to implement into your daily workflow, and it will increase your productivity without adding more hours to your day.

TIM BURCH, CR

Vice President, Middleburg Office, BOWA
Past President/Chairman, NARI Metro DC
Lead Project Manager, Extreme Makeover Home Edition, ABC Television

I was exposed to the system as a new general manager at Case in 2003, and it changed my life. Mark's system allowed me to be more strategic and proactively take control of my day. Additionally, some side benefits included reducing my stress and keeping all my promises both at home and work. I must admit I am guilty of using these techniques on the weekend to make sure the important things get done when it comes to fun.

STEPHEN SCHOLL, CR, CKBR

I have been using Mark Richardson's Time Mastery system for over fifteen years and find it invaluable. While it has evolved over time to meet my personal needs and style, the fundamental principles have remained the same. What I love about the system is not just how it provides a mechanism to ensure I stay on track and meet deadlines in a realistic manner, but how it gives me the chance to really think about how I'm using my time and how much time I'm devoting to each "bucket," or area of focus I need to tackle each day. It allows me to think beyond the immediate tasks at hand by also incorporating big-picture goals into my plan.

MICHELLE DOISCHEN

President, Samantha Jordyn Marketing, LLC

CONTROL YOUR DAY

BEFORE IT CONTROLS YOU

CONTROL YOUR DAY

BEFORE IT CONTROLS YOU

THE 7 STEPS
TO MASTERING YOUR TIME

MARK G. RICHARDSON

Published by Advantage, Charleston, South Carolina.
Member of Advantage Media Group.

ADVANTAGE is a registered trademark, and the Advantage colophon is a trademark of Advantage Media Group, Inc.

Printed in the United States of America.

10 9 8 7 6 5 4 3 2 1

ISBN: 978-1-59932-899-7
LCCN: 2017946368

Cover and layout design by George Stevens.

This publication is designed to provide accurate and authoritative information in regard to the subject matter covered. It is sold with the understanding that the publisher is not engaged in rendering legal, accounting, or other professional services. If legal advice or other expert assistance is required, the services of a competent professional person should be sought.

 Advantage Media Group is proud to be a part of the Tree Neutral® program. Tree Neutral offsets the number of trees consumed in the production and printing of this book by taking proactive steps such as planting trees in direct proportion to the number of trees used to print books. To learn more about Tree Neutral, please visit **www.treeneutral.com.**

Advantage Media Group is a publisher of business, self-improvement, and professional development books. We help entrepreneurs, business leaders, and professionals share their Stories, Passion, and Knowledge to help others Learn & Grow. Do you have a manuscript or book idea that you would like us to consider for publishing? Please visit advantagefamily.com or call **1.866.775.1696.**

To all those who have made mastering time a priority.

ACKNOWLEDGMENTS

. . . .

Writing an acknowledgment feels like writing your own obituary. Whether you have written a book or not, an acknowledgement is more about an author's reflections than communication to the reader. Those who know me (very few of you do) know I am very passionate about learning and listening to new ideas and insights. These can come in many forms and from many directions. So I will attempt to acknowledge those who have been important in the time-mastery journey.

I begin with my parents, James and Sheila Richardson, who laid my life's foundation, which is both solid and wide reaching. They created an environment for learning and experimentation and a big safety net to reduce risks.

I also want to acknowledge Thomas Regan, my architecture advisor at Virginia Tech and my first true mentor. Professor Regan taught me how to think through the language of architecture. He pushed me to see the world through multiple lenses. He gave me a methodology that could be translated into many areas of life (including writing).

Next is Fred Case. Fred created a landscape where I could flourish and grow. The results of this growth and accomplishment have allowed me to expand my reach and help others touch greatness.

In addition to this foundation, I want to thank my wife, Margie, and my kids, Jessica, Jamie, and Brett. They are my "why." They keep me grounded and humble. Margie pushes me to excellence when good may have sufficed.

I also want to acknowledge a few advisors who have inspired me to push the teaching of time mastery to the place where I can write this book: first, Bill Baldwin (my first student); then, Tammy Ruffin, Steve Scholl, Rob Patterson, Michelle Doischen, Laurie Griel, Melissa Kennedy, Beth Yuen, Anthony Nardo, Mary Miksch, Sam Imhof, Tim Burch, Bill Millholland, Jeff Miller, Tim Walker, Homa Nowrouzi, Sam Imhof, Keith Vaughn, Shashi Bellamkonda, and Jonathon Katz; and, last but not least, all the others who have consciously or subconsciously given me concepts, ideas, and inspiration.

TABLE OF CONTENTS

INTRODUCTION

"I wasted time, and now doth time waste me."

WILLIAM SHAKESPEARE

Time. It's a simple concept. Anyone can tell you the time of the day. Or they can tell you the number of hours in a day or days in a week. Time is something we can quantify in a consistent, numerical way. We can measure it and use it to compare. We communicate about time every day. Most people get paid based on the amount of time they work. This is all very straightforward. But if you ask the same people to explain what time *means* to them, the answers vary because even though time is very simple to understand, it is hard to control or master.

I became interested in the subject of time in the late 1980s. I was feeling overwhelmed and stressed by all the balls I was juggling. A friend suggested that I take a time-management course. I found a one-day seminar taught by a University of Maryland professor. The morning was spent discussing time on a very long-term level—ten years and beyond. The professor had us do exercises to visualize what our lives might look like in ten years. After lunch, we began drilling down into the five-year perspective, then one year, then one month. The last hour of the class was spent focusing on planning one single day. It seemed very logical to evaluate time on a macro level and then work our way down to the micro level of daily tasks. I remember coming away that day feeling stimulated intellectually. However, I did not know how to apply what I had learned the next day. Like other failed attempts to improve something, I just went back to my old patterns and routines that did nothing to reduce my stress.

The pain I was experiencing from overwhelm was not going away, and my thirst to do more only made it worse. So I decided to crack the code on my own. Because my background is in architecture and design, I have always found that diagramming and making things visual helped me understand them better. I, like many others, had been making "to-do" lists and had been taught to prioritize and focus on the tougher things first. While these simple techniques made sense, I still felt crappy at the end of the day unless several things were crossed off my list.

Using my architectural thinking process, I decided to approach this daily exercise as if I were designing a project. First, I needed to identify all the "givens" or "ingredients." This is like compiling a "to-do" list. After doing what I call a "brain dump," I could visualize the pieces. I would then try to analyze each item with more detail and estimate the amount of time each activity should take. I would add the total amount of time for all the tasks and would see how that compared to the time available in a day. At first it was difficult to get this to match up, but with practice, I became better at it. I also needed a way to visualize my day. Since I was proficient with timelines and Gantt charts from construction projects, I simply used these same visual tools.

It was a learning process, but I developed a system that began to save minutes here and minutes there—and people began to notice. In 1991, I had a project manager ask me if I could teach him my time-management strategy because he saw the difference in my productivity and wanted to have the same. He began to use my techniques and tools successfully and then told several others in my company how he learned to get his days under control. That led to my giving a time-management seminar for my company. Word about my successful visual techniques spread throughout local and national associations, and I became sort of a go-to speaker on the subject. I became the architectural thinker with the design-based system to take control of your day.

Over the past twenty-five years, I have presented this topic to more than ten thousand people. I would *like* to tell you there are ten thousand users of my techniques, but that would not be true. I will say, however, that most people do look at time a little differently now. Most have a yearning to constantly improve time effectiveness. I can only guess, but I would estimate that 10 to 20 percent of the attendees use these techniques daily and reap benefits such as accomplishing more, feeling less overwhelmed, keeping promises more consistently, and thinking more clearly.

I cannot promise you will buy into or use these techniques, but I can guarantee this process works for most people if they follow it closely. Many people have gone from being frustrated to being in control of their days and thus being more fulfilled.

This book focuses on your time mind-set; gives you the actual tools, tactics, and techniques of time mastery; and helps you create successful habits. So let us begin this time-mastery journey together.

UNDERSTANDING TIME

"Time is an illusion."

ALBERT EINSTEIN

I f you want to excel or improve in an activity or discipline, you need to first begin to invest some energy in thinking about it and understanding it better. This understanding not only leads to an opportunity to master it but also to embrace it and enjoy the process.

It is hard to enjoy watching a football game if you don't understand the number of points a team receives when it makes a touchdown. It is also difficult to appreciate this sport if you don't know the basic language the commentator is using to describe different roles on the field.

While you have lived with time all your life there are still some important concepts and themes to understand better, which I present in the following chapters.

CHAPTER 1

EFFICIENT VS. EFFECTIVE

*Every day is a bank account, and time is
our currency. No one is rich, no one is poor,
and we've got twenty-four hours each.*

CHRISTOPHER RICE

Mastering time involves being both efficient and effective—not just one or the other. When you understand each of these better, you can marry them and see the ideal outcome or balance. Let's begin by looking at some simple definitions of each.

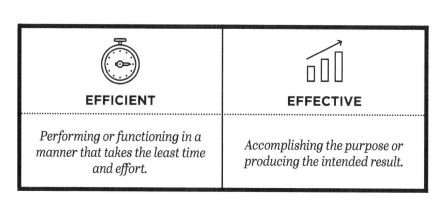

EFFICIENT	EFFECTIVE
Performing or functioning in a manner that takes the least time and effort.	*Accomplishing the purpose or producing the intended result.*

Many people use these words interchangeably, but they really have important differences. I often will look at how someone is doing a task or an activity and ask if it is being done in the least amount of time. I think nobody wants to waste time, so we often judge the success of an activity at least partially by how efficient we are in doing it—the amount of time it took.

Others might judge the success or failure based purely on whether you accomplished the goal.

Let's use a simple example that will illustrate the differences and how you might marry the two.

Bob needs to go to the grocery store on his way home from work to pick up some food for the family dinner. He jots down a quick list as he is sitting at the red light. He parks very close to the entrance (in a loading zone) and leaves his blinkers on. He runs into the store, grabs a handbasket, and quickly throws the items from his list in the basket. He is back in his car in eight minutes, ready to head home. He gets home and, while he got all the items on his list, he had not thought about needing a bottle of wine to go with the meal. He then makes the meal in an efficient manner and is done with the dinner by 7:30 p.m. Was this efficient? Most would say yes. Was it a great meal? Most would say "not really." While it fulfilled his hunger, it was not a memorable dining experience without the wine.

So imagine the scenario this way: Bob arrives at the same store without a list and parks out in the middle of the parking lot. He is not 100 percent sure what he will be buying, so he gets a large shopping cart. He knows he wants to grill something but is not sure what it is. So he begins at one end of the store, seeing if something will inspire him. As he strolls along, he bumps into an old friend he has not seen for six months. They have kids at the same school, so he catches up on the latest news. After about twenty minutes of catching up, he sees the store has some interesting fresh fish. There is a woman buying some, and he asks about the catch of the day. She says she finds this may be one of the best values in the store, shares how she found a recipe online, and describes how she grills this to make it an amazing meal. Bob decides that this really fits the bill and buys some too. Bob proceeds past the wine area and finds that his favorite wine is on sale, so he decides to stock up on a few bottles. After being in the store about forty-five minutes, Bob checks out and heads home.

Bob then dives into preparing the meal with his favored wine. Over dinner he shares his new insights about the school and completes his dinner about nine p.m.

These stories help to illustrate being efficient versus being effective. You could say in the first story Bob is more efficient; but is he more effective? Did he do it?

Not really. If Bob had taken a few minutes to think about the direction the meal might take or asked about other things he could accomplish or buy while he was at the store, he might have had a great meal, picked up a few school insights, and replenished his wine cellar.

In the second scenario, could Bob have done some things to be more efficient? I think you would say the answer is yes. However, with all that he accomplished, was he more effective? I would say yes.

It is important not to see planning as being mechanical or robotic. If Bob had spent five minutes doing a brain-dump list, shortened the conversation with the friend (and set up a time to chat further), and called home to get the grill started, he might have been finished with the whole process by 8:15 p.m. and had a wonderful meal with all the latest intel on the community.

I generally find that—when it comes to basic efficiency and effectiveness on activities and tasks—if I don't know the answers, I like to at least ask questions, such as the following:

1. **Is there another way to do this that might be more efficient or help in accomplishing other interests or goals?**

2. **Is there a way to leverage this activity into accomplishing more than just one task?**

3. **Can I multitask while doing the mundane parts of this activity?**

4. **Is there an opportunity to learn or experience something new?**

5. **How can I also think two or three steps ahead and be better prepared?**

6. **How much time will this take? Is there a way to save five or ten minutes?**

7. **Does this activity or task help me to achieve my medium- or long-term goals?**

By understanding the topic of being efficient versus effective, you will be better at balancing them both. By asking yourself and others questions, you will unleash the greatest computer in existence (your brain) to come up with better ways to do things. As you move along this journey to be more masterful of time, you will find that a higher level of sensitivity is a step toward that goal.

TIME MYTHS

Faster is better. No, *better* is better. This is especially true when it comes to time. I have a friend who always schedules meetings for twenty minutes. His thought process is good, but seven out of ten meetings result in incompleteness or in being rushed. I often find the crown jewels are in the little gaps of time or the little extra breathing room. I recommend setting the amount of time you think you'll need (e.g., twenty minutes) then adding just a little time (say five to ten minutes) for that extra cool idea or interaction.

CHAPTER 2

PROACTIVE TIME VS. REACTIVE TIME

*Time is the most valuable thing
that a man can spend.*

DIOGENES LAËRTIUS

While we are all given the same twenty-four hours in a day, one of the big differences is whether or not we are controlling the *use* of our time.

One way to begin better understanding time is to put our available moments into two separate buckets. The first is the time that we control (what I would call *proactive*). This is the time that goes into deciding what you are going to do along with the amount of time you want or need to devote to doing it. As you will read, the amount of time you decide to commit to something is often the time it takes to actually accomplish the task. It is a choice.

The second bucket is *reactive* time. This is time that you cannot control or that is controlled by others. We all have reactive time; however, the difference between people who are more masterful with time and those not very proficient with it is the percentage of proactive versus reactive time in their day. Understanding each more deeply will allow you to improve.

PROACTIVE TIME: TIME YOU CONTROL

Examples of proactive time might be the amount of time it takes you to do simple regular tasks like getting ready for work or eating lunch. If you determine that you need thirty minutes to perform a task like this successfully, then you allow the thirty minutes and move on with it. Other proactive time examples could involve a staff or client meeting or a project like writing an outline. You may need to be a little more flexible on what goes into the periods of time allowed, but if you estimate accurately, you should be proactive in that you control the amount of time dedicated to a task.

Another reason that the amount of proactive time is important is that you can *plan* it. You have a choice to spend less or more time to improve effectiveness. You can get creative with proactive time and find ways to reduce it or squeeze more out of it for a better return on your investment.

Reactive Time: Time That Others Control

We all know what reactive time is. Some common reactive activities include getting caught in a traffic jam or spilling coffee on a shirt and needing to change it. This may seem overly simplistic, but things like this happen throughout any day and we cannot plan for them. Other reactive activities, such as interruptions by clients or team members, throw us off our proactive plan—and are things that we can potentially control better. I have found that there is a basic but big cultural difference between those businesses that have a great deal of reactive activity and those that have much less. While reducing it and controlling it is important, I think allowing for the right amount of reactive dynamic is also where some creative ideas and deeper relationships are built.

As you begin to understand this subject a little more, I suggest you take a quick inventory of your day or week. Such an inventory can be done by asking two simple questions, then taking time to do some analyses to validate your gut.

Question one: What percentage of your day or week is "proactive"?

———————

Question two: What percentage of your day or week is "reactive"?

———————

While there is no right or wrong blend, I have found some truisms:

1. The higher the percentage of proactive time, the better.

2. People who accomplish more generally have a higher proactive percentage.

3. Your job or role in a business has some effect on the blend. (e.g., a receptionist has a high percentage of reactive time, while a manager ideally should have a low percentage of reactive time).

4. If your proactive number is less than 85 percent, you can generally improve it with the right mind-set and techniques.

5. By following a daily planning system, you can dramatically improve this blend.

The time-mastery system will give you a tool to improve in this area; however, there are three primary sources of reactive time for most people. If you begin to recognize these sources, you can immediately begin to improve and shift some of the reactive time toward being more proactive.

1. **Your clients:** Reacting to client needs is important for any client-centric organization, but you can develop a win-win dynamic with respect to reducing reactive time. Generally, while they may appreciate your willingness to react, it may not give them the best advice or outcome. While this may seem overly simplistic and general, I think you can adopt the following steps into your world or situation:

    a.   On Monday morning ask yourself, "Whom would I like to interact with this week? Who might have an issue arise that I will need to address?"

    b.   With a list of clients or client situations, proactively connect to each with a simple e-mail or text: "John: I know there are a few loose ends on your project that need attention this week. Would you be available on Wednesday at noon (or at 3:00 p.m.) for a twenty-minute catch-up call so I can help with these and any other questions you might have?"

    c.   As you get answers back, you can lock these times in on your schedule and move them to the proactive-time bucket.

Generally, I find you will get four or five out of ten clients going along with your respectful desire to be proactive. You will get two or three who don't care. Then you will get two or three who won't give up their desire to control you and may actually add to your reactiveness. Over time you will see a 50 to 75 percent improvement, which could change your 50 percent reactive and 50 percent proactive blend to 60/40 or 65/35.

    2.   **Your team/coworkers:** Being interrupted by your team with a question or an issue that needs your attention can be a big source of reactive time. People who end their day wondering what they got accomplished that day are generally a sponge for this type of reactive time. The question I asked myself many years ago was "Am I really

giving them the respect they deserve when I am interrupted and annoyed?" No. So the following is a process to consider:

a. When people interrupt you, ask if you can get back to them at a specific time to address their questions/issues.

b. If they say okay, make sure you keep your promise.

c. If they say no, ask them for the specific amount of time they need at that moment (and make them keep the promise).

Of course, there are some fires that need to be addressed immediately. However, out of ten interruptions, at least five will say they can wait; two to three will need addressing immediately; and two to three will vaporize because they came up with solutions themselves. Even a small shift of 5 or 10 percent of your time becoming more proactive can lead to a major shift over time.

3. **The family:** I think you can use the same methodology with your family; however, try not to be too mechanical or controlling. I am often asked about the difference between the weekday and weekend planning—and the biggest difference is the percentage of reactive time. On weekends, I generally surrender more of my time to my family's control.

The key to this theme is not just about getting the percentage of proactive time higher. It is about reducing the stress that reactiveness causes. It is about neither accomplishing more nor being constantly interrupted. It is about feeling better and more fulfilled at the end of the day. If you can begin to embrace this concept and start practicing some of the techniques, you will find the time-mastery system an easy way to build on your success.

CHAPTER 3

• •

FINDING THE CADENCE

*There is more to life than simply
increasing its speed.*

MAHATMA GANDHI

S uccess or failure in baking depends upon mixing the right ingredients together. It also depends on "how" the ingredients are mixed and "how long" something is baked in the oven.

While the concept of time may be a little elusive, the more you study the "how," the more masterful you will become. In the coming chapters, we'll talk about ways to make time more meaningful and easier to visualize in the coming chapters. But first, it's important to understand how you use the time you have.

To begin, it's important to understand time *rhythms*. This topic can be analyzed many ways, but let's focus on three particular rhythm questions that are important to mastering time.

1. When is the right time of day to do this?

2. When is the best time of day for my energy and mental state to do this activity?

3. How long should I invest in this activity today?

Most people have times of the day when we are more effective at accomplishing certain activities. Unfortunately we cannot always control when things need to get done, but with the right discipline, we usually can make a big difference in our planning. For a personal example, I find the best time to reflect on goals or long-term ideas and plans is very early in the morning. That is when my mind is strongest, allowing great ideas and thoughts in. It can be a very meditative time. Midmorning is when I usually feel most creative. That is when I schedule time to write, work on talks and podcasts, or move project concepts forward. Midday I am better at focusing on relationships, presentations, and conversations, so I use that time to focus on doing webinars, meetings, and conference calls. The last leg of my day is generally best for busy work or more methodical activities. This is not meant to be robotic, but knowing and understanding these mental cycles or rhythms helps me be more effective.

How does your day break out?

TIME OF DAY	Your Cycles in the Day	
	MIND-SET	ACTIVITY
Early Morning	Reflective	Planning
Midmorning	Creative	Projects
Lunch		
Afternoon		
Late Afternoon	Listening	Conversing
Evening		
Late Evening		

Break your day into five to eight parts. For example: early morning, midmorning, lunch, afternoon, late afternoon, evening, and late evening.

Then describe your mind-set and the type of activities you want to accomplish in each portion of your day. For example, very early: meditative/planning—exercise; midmorning: creative thinking—develop new project ideas.

You will use this knowledge to help determine the timing of different activities as you get deeper into the planning system.

TIME MYTHS

"There is not enough time for *x*." This is not true. You may choose not to invest the time, but the amount of time does exist. Generally, I try to get people to think first about the importance of a task and then try to quantify the amount of time for its successful completion. Then you can plan and find the time in the day to do it. I was doing a workshop with a group in California where the manager said he did not have time to take inventory and develop an improvement plan for his seven team members. I said, "Okay, can we do a simple timed exercise?" He agreed.

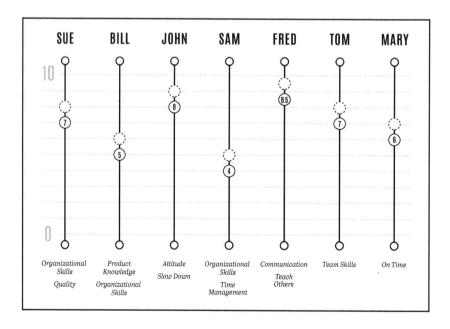

I asked him to give me the names of his seven team members. I wrote down the names on the flip chart. I then asked him to score each one on a zero-to-ten scale on the present overall effectiveness in their job; I added this next to their names. Then I asked him to give me one to three things that each member could do to increase his or her score by one point. He then shared the ideas. Then I stopped the clock.

This process took four minutes. He got my point. (I hope you do too.)

I have found there is almost always enough time for anything we have to do, if we just choose to do it properly. Always try to quantify— then decide how to make it happen.

Another important aspect of time cycle involves *when* is the best portion of the day to accomplish goals or be more effective. If you want to have people focused for a staff meeting, what is the best part of the day for them? If you need to do simple calls, can they be done while you are in your car or in between meetings? I often find "one-on-one" discussions that need a more relaxed dynamic are often best done over lunch or breakfast.

The third time cycle to consider is the length of time to invest into moving a project or task forward. Later, we discuss some basic time-estimating concepts, but this relates more to understanding and unpacking the right things at the right time. For example, you have three weeks to prepare a presentation for a meeting. One approach is to carve out a big chunk of time, knock it out completely, and be ready a week or two early. A better approach might be to break the preparation into parts. Begin with a thirty-minute brainstorm of some ideas for your talk. A couple of days later, share these ideas with a trusted advisor. A few days after that, spend thirty minutes writing a content outline and some key action items. A few days later, dive in and begin to put the parts together in a rough draft. Then you might get some feedback from colleagues. Finally, about four days before the presentation, you will be ready to wrap up a killer presentation. You will have also managed to move the presentation preparation along effectively while still addressing the many other activities in your days and weeks. Moving things too quickly or too slowly is not effective, so it's important to think about the "how" not just the "what."

JONES PRESENTATION = 6 HRS

vs.

JONES PRESENTATION =

Day 1	Brainstorm	30 minutes
Day 2	Discuss Approach	60 minutes
Day 3	Outline	30 minutes
Day 4	Draft Presentation	90 minutes
Day 5	Feedback	60 minutes
Day 6	Final Presentation	60 minutes

This leads to the concept of *cadence*. This is important in sports such as running or cycling. Finding the right cadence can be the difference between winning and losing. I learned this the hard way years ago in a cycling race. As an inexperienced cyclist (but in good shape), I started the race at a very strong pace ahead of the pack. Feeling confident, I thought if I kept up this pace I would have a great race.

About 75 percent of the way to the finish line, I ran out of gas, and I ended up with a very mediocre time. As I became better trained, I began to race based on the right heart-rate cadence. I also began to take on food and fluids at the right time, whether I was hungry or not. Knowing the right racing cadence not only improved the time but also allowed me to enjoy the ride more.

This theme holds true in mastering not only your time but also how you communicate time to others. A question I often ask myself or others is "Is this time allowed aggressive but realistic?" *Aggressive* means not being lazy or slow. *Realistic* means it can be accomplished in the amount of time available for completion without sacrificing other important tasks. If you consistently ask this question, you will get better at both hitting the time allowed and communicating and having others fit into your timetable. A simple metaphor that visually illustrates this theme is a rubber band. If it is limp—**not aggressive**—it does you no good. If you pull it too far—**too aggressive**—it will snap. If you give it the right tension—**aggressive but realistic**—it functions very effectively.

AGGRESSIVE BUT REALISTIC | *The Rubber Band*

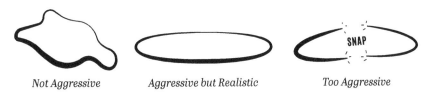

| Not Aggressive | Aggressive but Realistic | Too Aggressive |

Time mastery, in some ways, is like putting together pieces of a jigsaw puzzle, and cadence is one of the most important pieces. If you can focus on when is the best time and question how long something should realistically take, you will be much closer to being able to see the big picture.

CHAPTER 4

SAGE THOUGHTS ON TIME

A s I try to get my head around any topic or subject, I often find it helpful to seek out what other thought leaders have said about it. Generally, if something is said in an interesting, clever, or unique way it helps you think about a subject differently and gain some additional insights.

Here are quotes about the subject of time and some of my takeaways.

Time has no meaning in itself unless we choose to give it significance.

LEO BUSCAGLIA

By putting a spotlight on time, you elevate its importance or give it significance. You also will understand it better and can find ways to leverage it better. It is a choice.

A man who dares to waste one hour of time has not discovered the value of life.

CHARLES DARWIN

Well, we have all wasted time but those who waste less time generally value time more.

Time is money.

BENJAMIN FRANKLIN

Is time really money? Not really. Is there value in time? Sure. What I like about this simple quote is that if we translate time into something else, we learn to appreciate it more. In a later chapter I take you through an exercise to translate time into meaningful activities. After you do that, you will look at time (or wasting time) very differently.

Don't try to do tomorrow's work today.

FLORENCE NIGHTINGALE

It's important to know where you are heading, but if you don't put today's foot forward you will never get there. It is tough to stay in the moment, but with the right mind-set, the right system, and the right practice you will get there.

Time is what we want most but what we use worst.

WILLIAM PENN

We all have said, "If I only had time I would *x*." Or, "Where did the time go?" As I study the people who say these things the least, I find they are usually people who are masterful in understanding their time.

Work expands so as to fill the time available for its completion.

CYRIL NORTHCOTE PARKINSON

While it is important to not feel pressure to complete everything quickly, we tend to use all the time made available to complete a task. For example, if I go to the grocery store to pick up ingredients for a meal and I do not have time constraints, I will probably wander around the store while grabbing those ten ingredients. I might also say hello and chat with an old friend. I might even pick up a few more things while I am there. This task now takes about forty to fifty minutes to accomplish. On the other hand, if I give myself only twenty minutes to get the ten items, I will most likely avoid distractions and accomplish the same goal. Is the first way more relaxed? Maybe. But it took an extra twenty minutes. If I asked you what an additional twenty minutes each day would represent over the course of a year, you would be shocked. Would you trade adding a daily process to save you twenty minutes a day or 120 hours in a year? Most would say yes.

Fail to plan, then plan to fail.

BENJAMIN FRANKLIN

Most of us have some level of planning skills in both our personal and professional lives. These plans are generally a process we have been taught and have practiced. Some plans are simple, like planning a meal. Some are more complex, like planning a conference or designing a building. It is not very efficient to reinvent the wheel every time we tackle a meal or a project, so we follow a process. Ironically, we often don't have a written plan to follow and make the best decisions. The daily process and techniques you will learn follow this theme: if you can just invest twenty to thirty minutes a day, you will have a plan that will give you more control and clarity to accomplish your goals.

Plan your work and work your plan.

UNKNOWN

As noted, having a plan is important. But a daily plan (not just any plan) is critical to your success. Many years ago I heard an interview with a very successful man by the name of Mark McCormack. He was successful in business and his personal life. McCormack was a believer in daily plans. He said he spent about ninety minutes every day planning that day. He was methodical about his process and would not launch his day until the plan was complete and fine-tuned. The time-mastery process in this book provides a methodology to successfully design your day. Most will not spend ninety minutes, so it is designed to be done in twenty to thirty minutes. For the system to work, it must be done daily before you start your day. Then work your plan!

Yesterday is gone. Tomorrow has not yet come. We have only today. Let us begin.

MOTHER TERESA

While we have the complexity to reflect on the past and look to the future, this simple quote reminds us to live in the moment. It is about focusing intensely on today and then seeing the benefits of that success to build on tomorrow. The time-mastery system follows this simple quote to the tee.

Success is a verb.

DAN KENNEDY

Success is not a noun (even though most see it as a noun). When you realize that success comes from what you do, not what was done, you can control and master it. Just think, "Make it happen."

There are many other quotes or adages about time/success and inaction that speak for themselves:

The road to hell is paved with good intentions.

PROVERB

Practice makes perfect.

UNKNOWN

How did it get so late so soon?

DR. SEUSS

Time is the longest distance between two places.

TENNESSEE WILLIAMS

They always say time changes things, but you actually have to change them yourself.

ANDY WARHOL

These quotes and adages are like pieces of a jigsaw puzzle. They all fit together in an interesting way. If you look at just one piece you have a partial impression. But if you look at many of them joined together you gain an understanding and insight that is much more complete.

CHAPTER 5

HOW TIME HAS CHANGED

Change or become irrelevant.

Chris Edelen

A friend of mine won a major business award several years ago. In his acceptance speech he said, "If a business is not changing, it will become irrelevant." As I reflected on his words that day, I realized that irrelevance was the worst thing that could happen to a business (or a person). Just maintaining the status quo is not even an option anymore. Embracing how we look at time and how we control it is critical to constantly improving and remaining successful.

When I think about that speech today, it seems so much more relevant. Why is that—has time changed? For thousands of years, humans have recognized twenty-four hours in a day and seven days in a week. So the answer must be no, right?

Like many questions, though, you need to not only look at the "what" but also the "how." When we do, we see that time has changed in a number of ways even in our lifetimes, especially due to changes in technology.

TIME MYTHS

If I could sleep less, I could accomplish more. This was a misconception I had many years ago. I even made it a goal to sleep less. As I get older and wiser, I understand the value of sleep and rest more and more. Study after study has proven that sleep is not only about recharging, but it is also about subconsciously addressing important issues. It is also about buying time to make better decisions. The adage "sleep on it" is important for many reasons. I just encourage a little more proactivity with this subject. Generally, if you're really not sure of the best course, it is better to sleep on it. You can write down an item that you want to sleep on and put it next to your bed, and you will be amazed what the outcome can be.

HOW TIME HAS CHANGED

20 YEARS AGO		TODAY
TECHNOLOGY OPTIONAL	➡	DEPENDENT ON TECHNOLOGY
TIME BUILT VALUE	➡	TIME IS NOT ON YOUR SIDE
"FREE TIME"	➡	TIME IS NOT "FREE"
RETURN CALLS NEXT DAY	➡	RETURN CALLS THAT HOUR
"OFFICE HOURS"	➡	24/7
24 HOURS IN A DAY	➡	24 HOURS IN A DAY

TECHNOLOGY

For years, I have been telling the audiences at workshops and speaking events, "Technology will revolutionize business." I've recently adjusted this a little. Now I say, "Technology has revolutionized *everything*. We are living the future." Whether you embrace this technological wave or not, our real-time relationship with information has drastically changed how we manage our time. Today, technology is not an option; it is both an expectation and dependence.

BUILDING VALUE WITH TIME

 In the late 1980s, I told prospective clients that I would get back to them with design concepts in seven to fourteen days. This allowed us to organize our own workflow, and it also created a perception of value regarding the level of attention the project was getting—one to two weeks felt like a lot of value compared to the one to two days it takes now to do the same thing. Today, however, you win or lose projects by time. Speed sells. Conversion rates increase by the speed at which you can deliver. This happens in our personal lives too. Years ago, a restaurant's quality was often measured by how long you needed to wait to book a table reservation. Today, you pop in or call ahead for a restaurant and if they cannot seat you in a few minutes, most people move on to the next one. Scheduling a service appointment works the same way now: speed of service has become as important to many people as quality and price. While we often see value in the amount of time things take, time really is not on your side like it was years ago.

FREE TIME

 The concept of "free time" has changed drastically too. In the late 1990s, many people divided their time into three parts: work, family, and free time. You would ask new friends or even business interviewees what they did in their "free time." Today this language is not very common. Why? I believe it is because the voids or spare moments of non-work time have been filled with other activities, including more work. We are involved and have access to so many more things that the concept of "free time" has changed. Today, we talk about finding balance in our lives, but time is not a void that needs to be filled. If anything, for most people, the work hours aren't where the cup runneth over the most—it's the minutes when we are not working that are overflowing the most. Time is not *free*.

RETURNING CALLS

In the late eighties, my receptionist would tell clients that I would call them back within three business days. Then I changed the policy to always return calls within twenty-four hours; at the time, I thought this was a game changer for a client experience. Today, people expect you to return a call or an e-mail or a text *within one hour*. If it takes longer, many people instantly start wondering "Did they get my message?" "Should I be concerned?" "Should I move on and call someone else?" Now, you may not agree with this expectation, but if you can adopt this speed thinking, it can be very meaningful in business and in personal relationships. Think about how you feel if someone does not get back to you quickly.

OFFICE HOURS

In the early nineties, I treated most of my professional relationships like I would accountants or contractors. I would always ask, "What are your office hours?" With so many ways to reach people and our increased expectations about a quick reply, the question is now more open-ended: "When is the best time to reach you?"

Today, I sometimes get e-mails from my accountants or my editor as early as 5:00 a.m. or as late as 10:00 p.m. I would like to think this is about the importance of their relationship with me, but it is likely more about society's changing expectations about time. I am not proposing that you are "on" 24/7, but I think you would agree this is an example of how things have changed.

We can go on and on comparing things now versus then. Some elements of these changes are good—I like watching a season of my favorite television show without watching an advertisement, conducting conference calls from my car as I drive, or having basic supplies shipped in a day right to my front door. Other changes have only managed to add too many choices and additional stress for a lot of people. There have been many studies to validate the effects of the proliferation of choices and changing expectations. Many businesses have created value propositions primarily focused on speed (e.g., one-hour dry cleaning, one-day bath remodeling, one-day delivery, etc.). We often pay more for speed whether we need it or not.

While I think we can all acknowledge these changes, the difference in being successful is how we individually embrace these changes and how we become masters of time. We'll explore the "how"—the time-mastery system itself—in the second part of this book.

THE SEVEN STEPS TO MASTERING TIME

*A good plan is like a road map; it
shows the destination and usually
marks the best way to get there.*

H. STANLEY JUDD

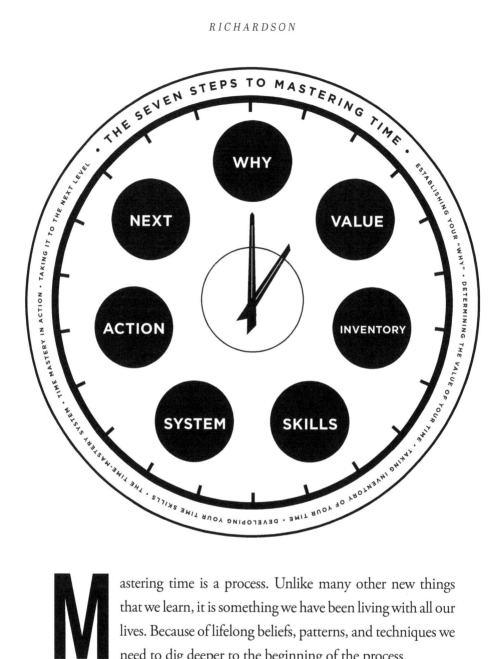

THE SEVEN STEPS TO MASTERING TIME

WHY • ESTABLISHING YOUR "WHY" • DETERMINING THE VALUE OF YOUR TIME • TAKING INVENTORY OF YOUR TIME • DEVELOPING YOUR TIME SKILLS • THE TIME-MASTERY SYSTEM • TIME MASTERY IN ACTION • TAKING IT TO THE NEXT LEVEL

WHY
NEXT
VALUE
ACTION
INVENTORY
SYSTEM
SKILLS

Mastering time is a process. Unlike many other new things that we learn, it is something we have been living with all our lives. Because of lifelong beliefs, patterns, and techniques we need to dig deeper to the beginning of the process.

There is not any special education or intellect required to follow this process. Like so many processes in your life, it is very logical and sensible. I have chosen the seven steps I believe are required for this journey. While I do not want you to skip any steps, I would not discourage you from adding a step or two if you think it will help you accomplish your goal of time mastery. While moving along this path, I strongly encourage discipline and focus. Many who attend my seminars fail due to falling off the process. By blocking out thirty minutes each day to do this process, you will not only fully understand it but also understand what is required to see success. Don't hesitate to use my other tools (recordings/webinars/visuals) to help deepen your understanding.

ESTABLISHING YOUR "WHY"

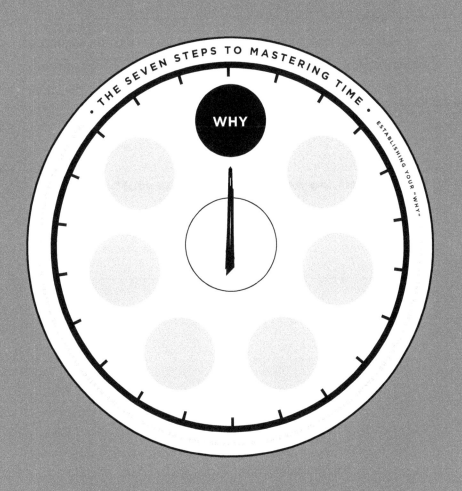

One of the most important questions people should ask themselves is "Why?" By asking this with almost any subject you gain both clarity and motivation.

For example, if you think you want to lose fifteen pounds, you probably have a good reason or two—but do you have enough reasons to actually go through the pain and inconvenience of making it happen? If you begin to list the reasons why you want to lose weight, you might find a pretty long list (including stamina, feeling better, cost of food, health, vanity, cost of health care, save on buying new clothes, pride, positive attitude, etc.).

This same methodology is true when it come to the subject of mastering time. When you begin to brainstorm a list, it is not only very motivating but it also begins to paint a picture as to the strategies and tactics you might want to focus on to master this topic.

So let's begin with making a list.

"Why is mastering your time important to you?"

1. _____

2. _____

3. _____

4. _____

5. _____

6. _____

7. _____

WHY IS MASTERING TIME IMPORTANT?

Over the years, I have asked audiences why taking control of their day would be important to them. Here are the most common seven reasons:

1. **Reduces stress.** Most people today are pretty stressed out. This stress is unhealthy on so many levels. If you have more control over your time, you will find that stress levels will go down.

2. **Allows you to accomplish more.** While this may not be your biggest motivation, accomplishing more is certainly nice. This could include staying connected to old friends or family or giving back to the community. Accomplishing more could mean doing a better job at any activity or task or making more money to invest. The bottom line is, if you have more mastery over your time, then there may be a little extra time in the tank for you to accomplish more.

3. **Allows you to think more clearly.** You are faced with many decisions every day. One characteristic of the most successful people is that they make fewer mistakes. Mistakes can be a product of not thinking things through, considering all the variables, and mapping out all the unintended consequences. By mastering your time, you can build in time to think more clearly too.

4. **Allows you to keep promises.** How do you feel when you don't keep your promises? They may be big or very small promises. Can others always count on you to come through 100 percent of the time with what you say you will do? While none of us are perfect, one byproduct of

mastering your time is keeping promises. As you reflect on people who keep or exceed their promises, you will find they are not only respected—but also quite successful.

5. **Allows you to focus on medium- and long-term goals.** Most people who struggle with time management spend almost all their time focusing on today or this week. They are reacting and putting out fires just to keep them from spreading. If you are spending most of your time only on the short term, you are compromising the longer vision and direction. Think about driving a car. Drivers who are enjoying the driving experience keep an eye on the immediate car and road around them, but they also appreciate the surrounding landscape and know where they are heading by looking out to the horizon to anticipate the weather or traffic ahead. This metaphor is relevant when you think about your time. By having control and mastery, you give yourself the license to adjust your focus, short, medium, and long term (and better enjoy the ride).

6. **Reduces overwhelm.** Overwhelm is a feeling that we all have experienced. It is not a good feeling. It causes stress, creates ineffectiveness, and makes us behave with others in an inappropriate manner. As I have studied this subject, I've discovered that it is quantifiable. Overwhelm is created by the proliferation of activities and variables. If you think about overwhelm like a juggler, you can start to understand it better. An amateur juggler can juggle three balls fairly easily. If you add a fourth or a fifth, he or she needs to concentrate more on keeping them in the air. If you add two more balls, then they all fall on the floor

and the juggler gives up in frustration. If you can think of activities that way, it helps in comprehending this theme. If you have only one or two tasks or activities to do, it is pretty easy not to feel overwhelmed. If you then add one or two more, or if you are interrupted by others adding more variables, then overwhelm begins to set in. By mastering your time and controlling the reactive time activities you will reduce overwhelm. (More to come on this.)

7. **Allows you to sleep better at night.** Some people may naturally not be very good sleepers. Most, however, lose sleep because of their environment. This environment could be noise or what you ate the day before. However, as I study this subject, I find that a high percentage of sleep loss is due to things that are whirling around in your head. It could be questions that need to be addressed or stress from deadlines. It also could be that you are trying to think through and organize activities for the next day. By mastering time you will give yourself the permission to shut down. You will be able to better focus in an organized way the next morning. All this allows you to get a better night's sleep.

KNOW YOUR WHY

There may be several other specific reasons why it would be great to master time. By keeping this why list top of mind, you will have the clarity and mastery to invest the time to get better at controlling time.

When you add all these up, the bottom line is you feel better and more fulfilled.

TIME MYTHS

I need to just get out of bed and dive into my day. I used to think this way. Now I try to stay in bed a little longer after I wake up. It may be fifteen or twenty minutes, but in that amount of time I can let the wave of the day begin to move though me. I can begin to visualize the day. I generally begin to feel the priorities or the positive or negative stress of the pace of the day that will need to be addressed in my plan. I now force myself to stay in bed for this amount of time. After I get out of bed, I find getting ready in the morning to be a more integral part of my planning process. While I brush my teeth or shave, I begin to filter the important questions that will influence my planning exercise. I also have the license to really stretch and think in longer-term intervals that may add a few actions to inch along. This reflective time after waking up is very important to creating a good road map for the day.

STEP 2

DETERMINING THE VALUE OF YOUR TIME

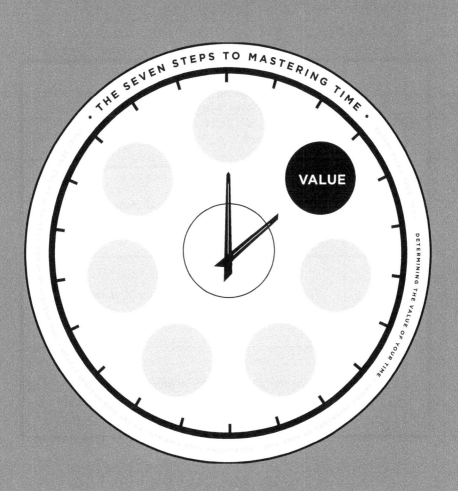

THE SEVEN STEPS TO MASTERING TIME

VALUE

DETERMINING THE VALUE OF YOUR TIME

As we discussed earlier, time is pretty elusive. We all have it, but we cannot see it. We can't touch it. We can't feel it. Time is the difference between winning and losing. Time affects whether we are poor or wealthy. Time is very important.

While I cannot sprinkle magic dust on it so you can literally see it, I can begin to give you ways and techniques to make it more meaningful and help you see its value.

One technique I use for audiences in workshops is to have them list different *amounts* of time. Then we try to attach an activity that is meaningful to them that can be done in that amount of time.

For example:

	Fifteen minutes might mean a short walk with your dog, getting ready for work in the morning, or stopping and grabbing a Starbucks coffee on the way in to work.
	One hour might mean an exercise class or watching your favorite TV show.
	Three hours might be a flight from DC to Denver or a drive to the beach.
	Eight hours might mean building a small deck, a day of work, or Thanksgiving Day with the family.

What do these time intervals mean to you?:

15 MIN.	
1 HOUR	
3 HOURS	
8 HOURS	
24 HOURS	

It is important that you find what resonates personally for you for each of these time frames. Then, as you engage in activities that require the same amount of time, (e.g., 1 hour = a staff meeting or a nice dinner with a friend) you begin to require and get the best use and value from your precious time.

By drilling into this deeper, you also push the envelope on what you can accomplish in a short amount of time.

For example, I was curious about how long it took me in the morning to prepare and make a pot of coffee. So I timed it. Initially it took about three minutes. Over time, I began to adjust the steps to be more efficient (and equally effective) and got the process down to one minute and a half. Now if you multiply this time out, I was able to save 9.1 hours in a year. Now what is the value and meaning of 9.1 hours? What can I do with 9.1 hours in a year? If it is billable time, then that is about $2,500. With $2,500 I can buy ten tickets for my wife and me to the Washington Nationals.

This is a simple (and maybe a little obsessive) example; but try to make the value of time more meaningful.

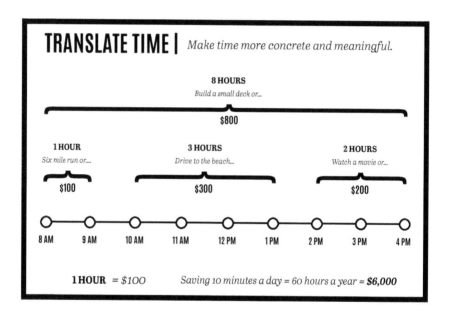

The key is first to really see the value of each minute. Then look at things you can do to improve these simple activities; and try to celebrate and use the windfall of the time savings in a positive way.

While this step is more of an awareness exercise, you will begin to look at and put more value in the time spent.

TIME MYTHS

Free time. Time is not free; stop using this phrase. If you begin to realize that you are generally just making a choice on how you invest your time—rather than not planning it—you will see time differently. As you become more proficient at measuring the value of time and comparing activities and the amounts of time they will take, you will stop using the term "free time." I like to blend and leverage professional and personal activities where you can get a lot more done with less stress.

TAKING INVENTORY
OF YOUR TIME

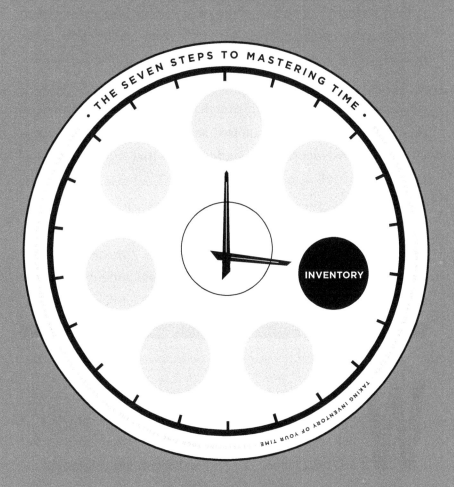

TIME MYTHS

I don't have time to exercise. Exercise might be one of the better things to do not only for your health but also to sharpen your time skills. If you have a limited amount of time, then begin with fifteen minutes a day. I asked a fitness expert, "If I only had fifteen minutes to exercise, what would you recommend?" He said, "Seven minutes of intense cardio, seven minutes of weights (or weight-bearing exercises), and one minute of stretching. I tried it, and really felt as though I'd had a real workout. Needless to say, I would encourage investing more than fifteen minutes, but if that is all you have at first, then start there. Another benefit of the exercise is that it gets the blood flowing in your brain to think more clearly and plan more effectively. My doctor explains how the nerve connections fire up when you exercise and you can supercharge the speed of your thoughts. So begin to think about exercising as a time-mastery tool and you will find the time to make working out a priority.

W hen you decide to improve on an aspect of your life, whether it's your health, relationships, or sports, it is important to take inventory of where you are now. For example, if you want to lose weight, you might want to evaluate your present caloric intake, the amount of exercise you get each week, and even the daily cycles and structure of your meals. When it comes to taking inventory of time, it may not be quite as tangible or obvious as your weight, but it is equally important and may even be more insightful.

Here are some ways to categorize time to help with your inventory:

1. Proactive time versus reactive time (see the earlier chapter dedicated to this): this is an important exercise to understand and it provides specific tips to set the stage for overall time mastery.

    a. Take a look at your calendar for the last few weeks and reflect on the amount of time you controlled versus reacted to.

    b. Think about an eight- or ten-hour day and the total number of hours that might fall into each bucket.

    c. Some days won't be typical, but try to get an average of a week or two. For example, if on Thursday you were in several meetings all day, then it probably was a high percentage of proactive time versus another day when you were putting out fires. If you average them together, it might give you 50 percent proactive and 50 percent reactive.

    As noted in the earlier chapter this is a foundational element, in that you first need to understand it, then take inventory, then commit to improving it if you ever want to master time.

2. Your other time blends (or time-portfolio blend).

    a. **Short-, medium-, long-term time:** While the ideal blend of time may vary depending upon your role in a business and where you are in your life, we all have the three levels of time. When you feel overwhelmed for an extended period, it is often from spending too much of your focus on short-term efforts only. It is like driving a car and only staring at the hood or just in front of you. It can be exhausting and not as productive.

Determine how much time you are spending on each interval of time. The three levels are defined as short term (this week), medium term (one to two months), and long term (two months or longer). They are sort of like micro versus wide-angle camera lenses. You can do a gut check based on the percentage of time you feel you spend on each, or you can drill deeply into the number of hours per week for each. After you take inventory of your present situation, begin to think about what would be ideal.

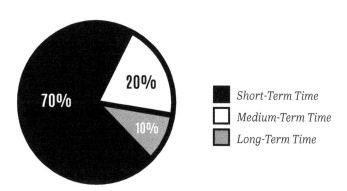

TIME SPENT ON INTERVAL EFFORTS: IDEAL WEEKLY BREAKDOWN

There are instances that require you to focus primarily on short-term time, such as moving a critical project through or putting a major fire out. However, in more normal cases, there should be an ideal blend. For most people, the ideal blend is about 70 to 75 percent short term, 15 to 20 percent medium term, and 10 to 15 percent long term.

b. **The diversity blend of activities in your week:** Another blend to evaluate is the percentage of time spent on the different types of activities in your week. By understanding this, you can begin to adjust it to be more effective and you can look for efficiencies in each. I generally recommend coming up with five to seven categories of activities in your week. For example: (1) meetings, (2) projects, (3) communications, (4) administration, (5) client interactions, (6) reactive time, (7) travel. Everyone has different categories, so don't let identifying the categories paralyze you. After you do this analysis a few times, fine-tune the categories to be more personally accurate and meaningful. Attach the number of hours or percentage of your time to each category in an average week. Set this analysis down and consider what your ideal percentage or blend should be. Compare the two and think about the gaps that need improvement.

BLEND OF ACTIVITIES (50-HOUR WEEK)			
	HOURS PER WEEK	**%**	**IDEAL**
Meetings	10		8
Projects	9		13
Communication	3		3
Administrative	4		3
Client Interactions	6		10
Reactive Time	10		5
Travel	8		8

c. **Work/family/you blend:** Another blend to evaluate is the blend of time you spend working versus with your family versus on yourself. Again, as I find when I am coaching business leaders, by asking this question you will find if you are in balance. You might be feeling resentful or frustrated. By taking inventory, you might reveal why. As an example, I did a deep dive into my travel schedule last year and discovered that the eighteen additional trips that had been added to my schedule took about 150 hours away from the time I had committed to myself and my writing. Thus, I was neither fulfilling my obligation to my publisher nor to myself. It was through this inventory that I could see, understand, and quantify the problem.

Your blend is a choice you control. I am not here to tell you what your blend should be. A good friend of mine believes you should only work as much as you need to fulfill your family's financial needs. Another friend finds his work a source of learning and cannot get enough of it. Finding your personal balance or blend is what is important.

How do you measure up to others? Do they think your balance is good, or can it be improved? This may be more subjective, but it will add to your understanding of the subject and give you clarity and motivation to adjust and change.

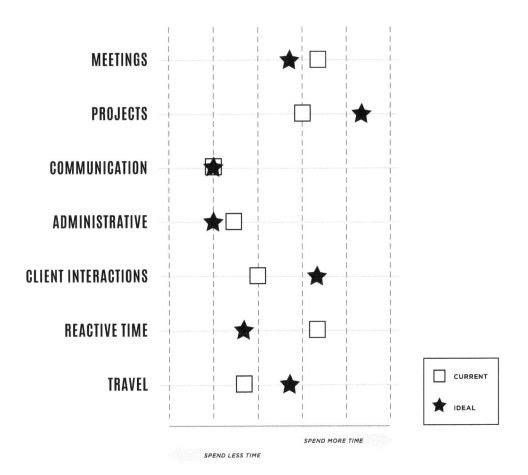

Try to find the gaps between actual time and ideal time. This is where you will see goals and ways to improve. For example, if you find your reactive time is above 20 percent, then begin to apply some of the tips that were discussed in the earlier chapter. If you are spending very little time on long term, begin by blocking out a sixty-minute appointment with yourself each week (just like you would with a client or team member) to plan for the long term. If your health is slipping because you don't have time to exercise, invest the time by planning and scheduling it.

We are all seeking balance. We all want to invest the right amount of ourselves in the right things at the right times. If you want to master your time, you must know where you stand now. Spend some time and have fun taking inventory. You will probably be surprised at the gems of time you might discover.

TOP-TEN TIME WASTERS

Time you enjoy wasting is not wasted time.

BERTRAND RUSSELL

As you become more conscious of time and make it a priority, you begin to realize that much of the success comes from three things:

1. Understanding it

2. Adopting and acting on new techniques and approaches

3. **Not doing things that waste time.**

When you quantify what makes the biggest difference, it might be less about adding new approaches and more about *eliminating* things.

Recently I heard someone draw a parallel of wasted time to a leaky faucet. If you don't fix the leak, over time you will have a big water bill. When we have a major pipe burst, we fix it quickly. However, the amount of waste or size of the water bill can be much greater with the drips than the burst. If you reduce or stop the drips of wasted time, it can have a huge benefit to achieve the success you yearn for. Remember, just ten minutes of drips of time per day equals sixty hours in a year.

The following are common time wasters. Maybe not all of them apply to you. Perhaps there are a few that you can tweak and you will see marginal improvement. Then again, there may be one or two that really hit a nerve and will make a big difference for you.

 1.   **Talking without listening.** Listening is a choice. Listening is a muscle that needs conditioning. Not listening wastes time. Think about people you know who are guilty of this. At times, everyone is guilty of talking too much—but at least try to recognize when you are doing this and practice "active listening." If you are focused on asking questions, then shutting up, you can get through a ten-minute conversation in five minutes—with a better outcome and clearer understanding of next steps.

 2.   **Not writing things down.** I know this sounds a little patronizing, but writing things down is not only about documenting; it is also about giving yourself permission not to have to remember. When you do not have to remember, you can

be in the moment. When you are in the moment, you listen and have more synergistic creative thoughts. If you don't write things down, you not only waste time trying to remember or needing someone to repeat, but also you are not opening up your brain to think ahead about your next move effectively.

 3. **Interruptions.** Interruptions exist for everyone. They exist at many levels (the power goes off in the office or you get a request for help from a team member). The reason these interruptions are a big time waster (and can be improved upon) is that we do not know how to react or deal with them. In the chapter about proactive and reactive time, I address this. If you can begin to control three or four of the ten interruptions a day, you will save hundreds of hours per year.

 4. **Not leveraging your time.** You are a very complex being. You can accomplish more than one thing at a time. I believe one time waster is doing simple required tasks and not leveraging that time to accomplish other things too. Some obvious examples are (1) driving, (2) exercising, and (3) eating. There are many others like walking the dog or waiting for a doctor's appointment or even watching TV. Now, you may choose not to leverage these, but you must at least acknowledge that there is an opportunity—by just doing a few additional simple tasks—to not waste time. For example, I make a list of calls so I can easily march through them on a twenty- or thirty-minute drive. Or I

use my exercise time to read a draft of a column or brainstorm a podcast topic. Multitasking is an opportunity to leverage time. If you look carefully at your day, you can find creative ways to leverage your time. It's a mistake not to use this time.

 5.   **Being late.** Being late is not only disrespectful; it also can waste your time. If you are late for a dinner reservation, you may lose your table. If you're late for a meeting, not only do you waste other people's time, the flow of the agenda may need to be repeated or shortened and rendered ineffective. Life would be so much better if you could count on everyone being on time. Successful people are not late!

TIME MYTHS

It is okay to be a few minutes late. Wrong. Masters of time are on time. They understand that being late not only is unprofessional but also can snowball and throw off many minutes in the day that they can never get back. There is an amusing quote that many Americans believe: "late + excuse = on time."

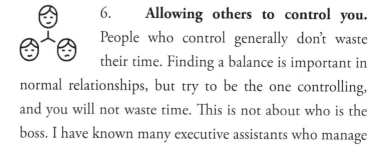

6.   **Allowing others to control you.** People who control generally don't waste their time. Finding a balance is important in normal relationships, but try to be the one controlling, and you will not waste time. This is not about who is the boss. I have known many executive assistants who manage up as well as down, and they don't waste time.

7.   **Being too slow or too fast.** Finding the right amount of time and the right cadence is important. In the absence of this, you can waste time. If you give yourself thirty minutes to pick up milk and cheese at the store when you could do it in fifteen minutes, your internal cycle will use more of the time and waste a few minutes. The flipside is also true in that, if you only give yourself ten minutes, you might make a mistake or need to go back for another trip. As you begin to master time you also master the cadence and pace to do things right with the right amount of time.

8.   **Not saying no (gracefully).** Most of us are pleasers who want to help others. Most of us believe when we are asked to help, saying yes is the best answer. I am not encouraging you to be unkind or unhelpful. I do believe, though, that always saying yes is a time waster for you. As you begin to quantify this, do some simple math. If with ten requests (personal or professional) you can just say no (or at least "not now") to two or three of the interruptions you are most reluctant to do, and with two or three ask if you can respond back in

an hour or two, you will get a big dividend in return. The key is to be graceful, kind, and effective.

9. **Doing things that you should not do.** If there are ten to fifteen things in the day that you do, I would be willing to bet that a few of those could have been eliminated—and that you would look back at them and say, "That was a waste of time." The best way to address this is to think more deeply before you commit to something. A few questions you might run through your filter are: (a) Do I really need to do this? (b) Is there a better way to accomplish it? (c) What is the worst thing that will happen if I don't do it? Again, the point is to not waste time. If you can eliminate a few of these ten to fifteen things, then you can use the time more effectively (even if it is just taking a nap).

10. **Not having a plan.** Think about jumping in the car and needing to make five stops but not planning your route beforehand. Or what if you are preparing a special meal for friends and you go to the grocery store without making a shopping list? You wouldn't dive into a remodeling project without preparing a sketch or a material list. The same is true as you move through your day. By not having a plan, you are sure to waste time. You will make mistakes. You will need to redo things. You will not be able to see some of the efficiencies in front of you.

What are your time wasters? List your top ten.

_____

_____

_____

_____

_____

_____

_____

_____

_____

_____

Use these strategies as a checklist. Rate yourself from zero to ten on each of these time wasters. Focus on improving one or two where you have the lowest scores. If you do, you will receive a priceless gift— time. This gift did not cost you any money, and it could give you a huge personal or financial return. Just stop wasting it!

STEP 4

DEVELOPING YOUR
TIME SKILLS

While some people may have the right motivation to become time masters, and others feel the need to change, the process also requires skills.

There are many examples of this in daily life, including sports. Regardless of how much you love the game of baseball, if you want to play well you need to be skillful in hitting, fielding, throwing, catching, and running. These may not require superman talents, but they are skills to master.

Successful time mastery also involves developing skills and ongoing practice.

The first belief is that 80 percent of time success is a science and 20 percent is an art. This is important to believe because you are giving yourself the permission to get better if you choose. You were not born to be a time master.

SUCCESS =

80% Science   *20% Art*

You can have the right beliefs and change what you are doing but you also need time skills to be successful. Planning is a skill.

Another important formula to become more skillful is: A + B = R

For many people, achieving success is an outcome. But those who achieve success realize that the outcome is just a product of doing certain things. The formula to achieve the success outcome is:

$$A \text{ (attitude)} + B \text{ (behavior)} = R \text{ (results)}$$

If you focus on the attitude and the behaviors the results will follow.

For example:

A (attitude)	=	the right mind-set
A	=	positive attitude
A	=	work ethic
A	=	discipline
B (behavior)	=	getting skills
B	=	gaining knowledge
B	=	following a process consistently
R (results)	=	the goal/outcome

Developing the right attitude and the right behaviors are just like working on any other skills. You just need to identify them and then work on a plan to improve them.

The following are some key skills for time mastery.

VISUALIZING TIME: IF YOU CAN SEE IT . . . YOU GET IT

Based on my experience training thousands of individuals in business improvement, sales, and marketing, I would say most people are visual thinkers. They understand better when they can visualize something. If I simply talk about basic concepts or processes, often I am met with glazed stares. If I supplement my talk with an image or a diagram illustrating the same concept, the comprehension and understanding increases significantly. And if they understand it, they can master it.

Visualization can involve very literal images, or it can be about tapping into our experiences through analogies or metaphors. The use of metaphors and analogies can help the person you are trying to communicate with understand more easily. For example, I talk about the four quarters of a football game. If a team is ahead twenty to zero after the first quarter, they are probably not going to abandon their game plan. On the other hand, if the halftime score is zero to twenty, the strategy dramatically changes. For people who understand football, they immediately get this concept of how urgency could affect how you look at time.

There are many visual experiences that relate to understanding time, such as driving speed or the dashboard on a car. It can also be wandering lost in a maze, not knowing where you are going and the inefficiency of that. Time-related analogies can also work with cooking or exercise (e.g., taking something out of the oven too soon).

Visualizations of time-related experiences.

The more you can visualize time and make translating time visually into a skill, the more you will be able to understand it, leverage it, and manipulate it to be more effective.

There are many other simple visual ways to think about time.

1. The traditional clock.

 By seeing time as a circle, you can comprehend an hour or a twelve-hour half-day better. There is a beginning and end. There is a cycle to it. Children need to see the numbers on a clock as a way to learn, but as people get older, most can begin to feel the time in quarter or halves or the complete circle. While very simple, it is a good example of making time visual.

2. Timeline.

 By visualizing time in a linear fashion, you see both the relationship (what needs to come first/middle/last) between activities and the volume of time each activity takes. Timelines are often used in days or weeks, but they can be equally effective on the scale of one day or even one hour. I like to use a "reverse timeline" when helping someone work though the activities and tasks required to achieve a deadline. By making it more visual and tangible, you can actually see how difficult or easy it will be to achieve the goal.

3. Calendar.

 With the advent of technology and the increased use of online scheduling, many people have gotten away from some basic uses of the printed calendar. A common calendar allows you to see the relationships of the day, week, month, and year. It also helps you measure how urgent certain tasks are and when you have blocks of time to work on things that might be overwhelming you. While I find new technologies helpful I also use a simple traditional day timer so I can better see the weeks and months visually.

4. A Gantt chart.

Another less familiar but common time visualizer is a Gantt chart (invented by Henry Laurence Gantt in the early 1900s). This tool is used to map projects that have interdependent activities. It helps the user see the flow of the project, identifies opportunities to save or reduce time, and highlights critical tasks that need to be accomplished at a certain time. Using methodologies like this in other areas not only helps give you a better result but also helps you further understand time and the relationships between activities.

5. A metaphor.

"If a picture is worth a thousand words, a metaphor is worth a thousand pictures." Most of us communicate daily using metaphors. Some people use them to be clever, but most use them to simply try to communicate ideas and themes. By thinking of metaphors that relate to time, you can visualize time better and therefore understand many of the impacts of time, such as urgency, importance of planning, and short-term versus long-term time. If you are a sports fan, find a time metaphor in football or tennis. If you enjoy cooking, begin to think of a baking or cooking metaphor that relates to time. Any area (like fishing or flying or driving) has potential metaphors that are useful in understanding and communicating time. Try to think of a few. Make a game out of it over dinner with your family and they will become more top of mind. The key to using metaphors is finding a relevant topic that will help you see and understand time better. And again, if you see it you will get it.

As you become more masterful with time-visualization tools, you will elevate your understanding. With greater understanding, time will become more important to you. And when that happens, your mental time muscles will become stronger.

ESTIMATING TIME

To become more masterful managing your time, you must condition your estimating time "muscle". I refer to it as a muscle more than a skill because, like muscle in your body, the more you use it, the stronger they become.

Being able to estimate time has several elements to it.

1. **A mind-set.** Begin thinking about how much time things take and visually connecting the dots between time and an activity. It will improve your estimating-time skill but also creates more meaning and value in the activity.

2. **Practice.** Like any other muscle, it needs to be active, not static or passive. Practicing time estimation can be painful or uncomfortable for some people. Like other physical exercises, once you do it regularly, it can be fun and fulfilling. You might even get the runner's (time estimator's) high if you work it.

3. **Courage.** When I ask people to estimate the time it takes for a task, one of the biggest obstacles is the fear of being wrong. When you are fearful of something you tend to be paralyzed and not do or think about it. I often then ask, "What is the worst thing about being wrong?" It's not really a big deal. So get out of your comfort zone and guess more, then see how close you are (it might even become fun). This courage will lead to being better and more skillful.

When I began my career in the remodeling business, I had to estimate the time many things would take. How long would it take to build a wall or tear out a bathroom? How much time would be required to design and develop a plan for an addition to a home? How many meetings would be required to make all the design decisions and come to closure on a construction contract? Estimating these activities not only made me more knowledgeable at estimating time; it also helped me develop the estimating-time muscles to apply it to other daily activities. Once you begin to really see the benefits of this subject, you practice it more, and you begin to have fun with it too.

The following are a few tips that will allow you to begin to sharpen your estimating skills and improve in this important time-mastery topic.

1. **Guess and then measure it.** Begin with some simple tasks like making breakfast in the morning, getting ready for work, or doing your exercise routine. While it may sound a little mechanical, write down the number of minutes you think it takes to do some routine tasks. Then check the amount of time it actually takes. For example, it takes me five minutes to make breakfast, and it takes me twelve minutes to do my morning routine. By beginning to do these simple time exercises, you will improve your estimating skills/muscles. After thinking about the simple daily tasks, expand your estimating: How long will it take for an effective meeting or for a project to be completed? Don't be paralyzed by fear of being wrong. If you guess, that will lead to being more knowledgeable, which will in turn lead to the confidence needed to estimate time. This is an important skill if you are going to master time.

2. **Question the amount of time it takes.** Ask yourself, "Are there ways to save time in this process?" Just by asking the question, you will not only be more conscious of the time but also should be able to find ways to improve and save some time. I was able to save ninety seconds in making my coffee, which is about ten hours per year. Don't get too obsessed by the questioning; but by asking, your knowledge and sensitivity in estimating time will increase.

3. **Make it a game.** I often will do time games with people when discussing subjects like this. Ask a family member or friend to estimate time for any familiar task. For example, "How much time does it take to watch a baseball game on TV without the commercials?" or "How much time does it take to shop at the grocery store?" This may not be a game where there is a winner or loser, but it does allow you to see how time-sensitive that person is or how good they are at estimating time.

4. **List things that take about the same amount of time.** Another exercise that helps improve your estimating muscles is to list a few amounts of time and then list three activities that roughly can fit that amount of time; for example: ten minutes = a short dog walk / a shower / calling my sister; thirty minutes = going and getting my hair cut / a longer dog walk / making dinner; sixty minutes = driving to work / a lunch with a business friend / a healthy workout; four hours = a drive to the beach / building a set of shelves / a movie and dinner. By beginning to estimate the time things take and then comparing them to others things, you not only improve the estimating skills but you also begin

to think about time in terms of equivalent activities. Do this with activities that are important to *you.*

5. **Make estimating time more visual.** As discussed earlier, I believe most people are visual thinkers. If you can begin to see the time visually, you can also estimate it better. For example, draw a line on a piece of paper. This line represents eight hours. Now make a circle at the beginning and then the end of the line and a circle in the middle so you now have two parts representing four-hour segments. Then add a circle just a short distance from one end. This now represents an hour. Now begin to see your day in this line. Begin to estimate activities that fit into the time slots.

Another way to estimate time visually is by using a pie chart, as discussed in the earlier chapter. The pie chart represents a day and can be used to estimate (and illustrate) the five to seven categories of activities (personal and professional) that will make up the day. Is this an ideal amount of time? Are there ways you can improve it or reallocate some time for other things? In a later chapter, I talk about a "stress-cloud" exercise later to help visualize and reduce stress. If you think about time as a cloud (estimating big chunks of time as big clouds that don't let the sun come in and small ones as just passing or scattered clouds), you begin to see not only why you are feeling the way you are (in a funk) and also ways to break up the cloud and let the sun come in. There are many ways to estimate time visually, but you just need to begin with drawing a line.

Not being able to accurately estimate time is like approaching the subject of time mastery in the dark or flying blind or trying to run a race with a broken leg. If you can become more conscious of how long things can take, you are on a good path towards becoming more masterful.

Three things to close with:

1. **Estimate it**

2. **See it**

3. **Control it**

Then you will begin to master time.

ANALYZING TIME

Another skill or muscle that you need to use and improve upon is analysis. This begins with asking the right questions. I generally encourage people to ask themselves these five questions to begin the process:

1. *Why am I doing this?*

2. *Is there a better way to do it?*

3. *Am I moving my longer-term goals forward?*

4. *Is there a way to delegate this effectively?*

5. *Is this an aggressive but realistic pace?*

After meaningful questions, try to use some visualization techniques and tools to see the answer.

For example, I did a deep analysis of the amount of time I spent traveling in 2016. I made, on average, three trips every two weeks. Some were short and some were longer. I then figured the amount of unproductive time relating to travel (cabs, security lines, an occasional delayed flight, boarding process, paperwork, travel arrangements, etc.) I determined that an average trip had seven hours of time that was unproductive (as well as stressful or boring). I then multiplied that by the number of trips (about seventy-five) in the year. This gave me 525 unproductive hours in the year. So I determined if I could reduce the number of trips to forty, I would save 245 unproductive hours. To express this in equivalent terms, in 245 hours I was able to write this book, develop a podcast series, and walk my dog three times a week.

Without this simple analysis, I would not have appreciated the wasted time and how I could invest it more positively.

This is a process. It's a skill that you need to develop if you want to be more time-masterful.

The analysis process:

1. **Take inventory of the numbers** (hours/ROI/blends).

2. **Ask the right questions** (write it down).

3. **Determine a solution** (diagram and make a plan).

The more you can make the analysis visual, the better you will see the road map to success. Once you have done this, you realize that by just investing the time to study the data you will glean important solutions and better answers.

TIME MYTHS

I need to set an alarm clock. Most people use an alarm clock—but I have not used one since 1992. When you become more acute at estimating time, you can just tell yourself when you need to wake up, and your body will do it for you. I am not sure how this works, but I do believe there are time muscles that we need to use. We especially see this in animals, like our pets. My dog Charlie wakes up at precisely the same time every day. He knows exactly when it is time (6:00 p.m.) for his dinner. Again, I am not a doctor or a scientist, but if you begin to consciously think about time, your ability to be aware of it and control it improves.

MAKING APPOINTMENTS WITH YOURSELF

While this is a simple act, it is also a skill and a habit. You may have heard the biblical commandment, "Thou shalt love thy neighbor as thyself." Some people read this and think it is about being nice and kind to others. However, it can also be interpreted as saying that loving yourself is important, too. While you might think of this as a mind-set more than a skill, I think the most successful people believe they are important—and you need to treat yourself with the same degree of reverence as you do others.

I make this part of the time-mastery process skills because, when we boil it all down, it is about making time for *you*. I include it in the planning process because if you don't make these appointments with yourself, improvement does not happen. We've been told it is strange to talk to ourselves—but talking to myself is critical to success. And I must admit I love making appointments with myself.

	SUN	MON	TUE	WED	THU	FRI	SAT
8 am		Plan next mo. sales targets					
9 am						Work on computer skills	
10 am							
11 am							
12 pm					Lunch with advisor		
1 pm							
2 pm							
3 pm							
4 pm				Develop top 10 ideas for summer			
5 pm							
6 pm							

You can make appointments (and block it out in your week and day) to do regular things like exercise or walk the dog. You can also make appointments (even small ones, twenty to thirty minutes) with yourself to focus on various ways you want to improve. I often create a meeting with myself to think about a topic or issue that needs attention, such as an issue with a family member or a team-member question to contemplate.

On a very practical basis I find it is best to highlight in advance a few of these mini-appointments. Then on the day-of brain dump, include this as an item: "Mark: top fun things for this summer." Then estimate the amount of time you want to think or work on this (say twenty minutes) and build it into the day's design just like you would any other item.

Because this is a meeting with yourself you should treat it as important as any other meeting—without interruptions, at a designated time, and with the thoughts documented.

Again some may say this is a mind-set more than a skill, but if you develop the techniques and fine-tune them, it is hugely valuable to feeling better and more fulfilled.

THE TIME-MASTERY SYSTEM

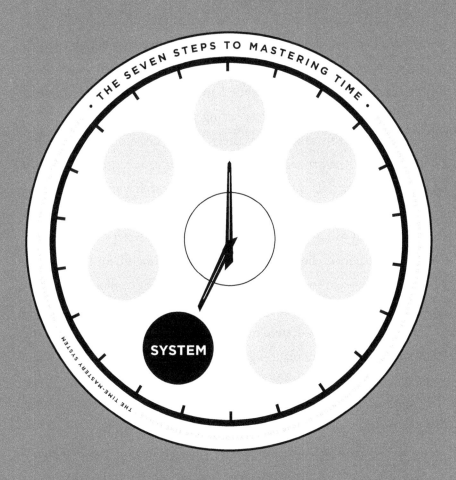

The future starts today, not tomorrow.

POPE JOHN PAUL II

n earlier chapters, I established the importance of time management. I have also given you new ways to think about time. Some
of you have already begun to take serious inventory of how you
are spending your time and where the opportunities for
improvement lie. This system pulls together everything you have read
so far. If you need to go back and skim the themes and chapters, it
might help bring the following time-mastery system to life.

Now this is where the secret sauce is. I will give you a system
to overlay these new thoughts and insights into an actual daily plan
or tool. The plan is a blueprint, like an architectural design, which,
when followed correctly, will allow you to accomplish more, keep
promises, and be less overwhelmed and stressed. The goal is to be in
control of your day rather than letting your day control you.

I refer to this as a time-mastery system because it is a step-by-
step process. The process has a specific order to the steps and it *must*
be followed in that order (in the same way that you don't preheat
the oven before you buy the ingredients). If you follow these steps
properly, you will get results. (Again . . . don't skip steps!) A pilot goes
through a specific checklist of steps before taking off, and this results
in a 99.99 percent success rate. It is also important to allocate the right
amount of time for each step. If you try to do this process too fast,
you will not get your desired outcome. There are important dogmatic
things, like doing the planning process in the morning, not the night
before, and finding a quiet place so you can concentrate fully. These
techniques and lessons have come from many years of experimenting
and coaching people who have adopted this successfully.

I also created a workbook that you can use for the first thirty
days. The workbook is like having training wheels while learning to
ride a bike. Once the system becomes part of your daily routine, you
can use your own spiral notebook. Again, this is a little dogmatic, but

it needs to be a spiral notebook. And you need to handwrite rather than use your computer.

There are several parts to the system, and I will walk you through them. First, read through the entire system to get an overview, then go back and use the book like a recipe to follow. There are other tools like the time-mastery system audio and video tools that can help you understand things better, connect the dots, and fine-tune your techniques.

THE TIME-MASTERY SYSTEM OUTLINE

1	THE SETUP
2	THE BRAIN DUMP
3	ESTIMATING THE TIME
4	TIMELINE SETUP
5	CONNECTING THE ACTIVITIES TO THE TIMELINE
6	ANALYZING THE PRELIMINARY PLAN
7	FINAL PLAN
8	LAUNCH
9	MONITORING THE JOURNEY
10	ADJUSTING THE PLAN

THE SETUP

The setup is the preparation step. This involves physical, environmental, and mental preparation. If you start the time-mastery system without the right environment, you will fail. If you don't have all your information for your day at your fingertips, you will create a weak plan. If you are distracted and not mentally focused when you begin, you will find the process painful and ineffective. Here are some basic keys for the setup step.

1. **Find a quiet place to do the time-mastery system (TMS).**
   It needs to be at the *beginning* of your day. If you do this process the night before, the design will be flawed. Things happen mysteriously overnight to change what your day's plan should be. The setting to plan could be in your home,

   your office, or even in a park or quiet corner of a coffee shop. If you do it in your home, it should not be at the breakfast table with your family. If it is in your office, you may need to find a quiet conference room to get away from the normal early-morning distractions at your desk. A friend who I once coached simply moved his setup location away from his office and became more successful with the system. If you're a person who works better at night, I recommend you create a to-do list at night and review it again in the morning.

2. **Have all your planning information at your fingertips.**
   This includes your calendar, saved voicemails, e-mails, text messages, and any other notes that might be useful. Think

of these as the ingredients you will assemble for a meal. If you are missing some, you will have a flawed outcome.

3. **Have enough time to plan.** I generally advise people to do the TMS at least sixty minutes before their first scheduled activity or meeting. For example, if you have a conference call at 8:30 a.m., make sure you are sitting down doing the TMS at or before 7:30 a.m. If your first meeting is at 10 a.m., you have some flexibility, but doing it at 7:30 a.m. is fine too. A rushed design is a flawed design.

TIME MYTHS

I don't have time to plan. This is one of the more common and painful misconceptions. I would say you don't have time *not* to plan. Planning is the key to finding large bonus dividends of time. Unfortunately, planning does take a little time. Some people try to do a daily plan in fifteen or twenty minutes and fail. You need a minimum of thirty minutes a day to plan. It is sort of like cooking time. Some things take thirty minutes to bake in the oven. If you take them out too early, they are not done and taste bad. If you leave things in too long, they will burn and also taste bad. By investing the minimum of thirty minutes, you will—after a week or two of using this system—realize a dividend of one to two hours of found time a day.

4. **Use the TMS notebook (or a spiral notebook).** While this may sound a little old fashioned, it is *critical* to your success. Most of the time when I follow up with students of the system who are struggling, I find it is simple things like not using a spiral  notebook that is derailing them. This notebook will be the blueprint that you carry with you throughout the day. It becomes a tool to document your thoughts so you can think more clearly and efficiently. Your TMS plan needs to be monitored frequently, and you need to have your notebook with you to do that.

5. **The first week or two will be awkward (and a little tough).** As I teach and present this system, most participants say it makes complete sense and they want to adopt it. Even people who struggle with the system initially will—after the first week—begin to see benefits like reduced stress and increased accomplishments. As with any lifestyle adjustment (like that first tough week of running), it takes time to instill new behavior. Try to be patient with the system and yourself.

THE TEMPLATE

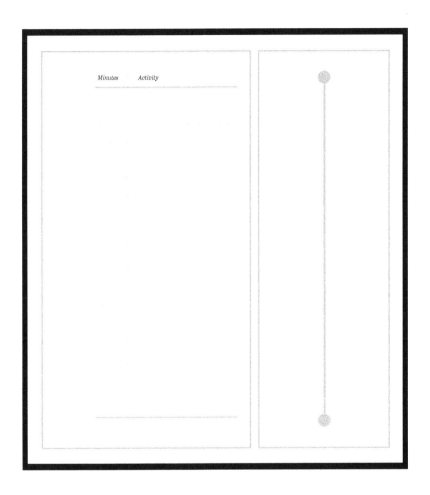

Minutes   Activity

*Success or failure is often determined
on the drawing board.*

R O B E R T M C K A I N

BRAIN DUMP

The brain dump is a deeper version of most people's "to-do" list.

To begin this process, I generally like to have a "theme" for the day. It can be philosophical like "be happy" or tactical like "close the deal." While some people find this less important, I find that having some directional theme for the day helps as you work through the planning process—and is helpful to keep you on track throughout the day.

Next, begin to do your brain dump (a deep to-do list). Write down as many personal and professional things as fast as you can that you need to do that day (and *only* that day). Your brain flows much faster than your hand can write, so try to abbreviate as you dump. Expand on each item as required with a couple of additional bullets that will help you understand the scope of what needs to be done, to help you better estimate the time later. If an item is a phone call, you might highlight a couple of things you want to discuss on that call. Have your calendar and other tools at your fingertips so that your brain dump can be very comprehensive. I am often asked, "How do you know when you are done with the brain dump?" It is simple. You are done when there is nothing left to dump out of your brain *for that day*. It is important to only list the items for that day. (If other thoughts pop up, just put them on a separate paper to add to your calendar for another day.) Over time this will become an easier and more natural process.

After you have somewhere between twelve and twenty-two items for your daily brain dump, take a brief "time out." Stand up; get a

Minutes	Activity
	Lunch
	Set... BM/JH/JA/MK
	Call John - SL Training
	JS mtg. sales profile system
	Meeting with Smith
	MK Card
	BM one on one
	Call GM; lease, trip, agenda
	Miller contract review
	ME B-Day
	Call Jim
	Set PM (Kit. Mtg.)
	Call Tom K (Oregon)
	CK w/WJFK schedule
	Call TB sales/vm/temp
	Reactive Time (Misc.)
	New Training Concept
	Set JR Lunch

Fig. 1 — Brain Dump

cup of coffee or a glass of water. Walk outside for a minute and get some fresh air. While you are doing this, ask yourself:

- *"Is there anything else I would like to accomplish today?"*

- *"Is there something in my longer-term plan I can inch forward today?"*

- *"Is there anyone else I can contact or help today?"*

By asking yourself these three questions, you will likely come up with a few additional items to add to your brain dump. Now you should have around fourteen to twenty-five items on your brain-dump list. If you have fewer than that, you might want to go a little deeper. If you have more, you might want to move some to another day or look for ways to combine/leverage them. At this point in the process, most people feel this is not hugely dissimilar from the to-do list process they currently do (just a little more structured).

Now add one very important item labeled "reactive time" to your brain dump list. I will explain this concept more.

Now the real planning starts.

ESTIMATING THE TIME

The next step in the process is to estimate the amount of minutes each task or activity will take. This process should be written on the left side of the brain dump items (see example). This is an estimation. Over time you will get better and more skillful at predicting time.

Use five minutes as the smallest increment of time, even for tasks that will only take a minute or two to complete. Try to be realistic with your estimates (not too conservative or liberal). If you are struggling or it is difficult to estimate, just guess—then use this as a placeholder to review a little later. The estimating-time step should only take five minutes. It may not be the same stream of consciousness as the brain dump, but don't labor over it. Just do a quick educated guess.

For example:

- *10 min. . . . call JR*

- *5 min. . . . set meeting with josh*

- *60 min. . . . meeting with SM . . . trip / DB / 2018 thoughts*

"Reactive time" is not something you can estimate. During the first thirty days, allow for 120 minutes of reactive time. This time is very important to plan for, but you cannot predict when it will happen.

Now add up all the minutes and write the sum down at the bottom. Then divide by sixty to give the number of hours needed to complete all the activities. Then compare that number to the overall hours available in that day. For instance, if it adds up to 9.75 hours and that day is 8:00 a.m. to 6:00 p.m. that equals ten hours—so it works! If, however, it adds up to twelve hours and you have ten hours

Minutes	Activity
20	Lunch
20	Set... BM/JH/JA/MK
30	Call John - SL Training
60	JS mtg. sales profile system
90	Meeting with Smith
15	MK Card
60	BM one on one
30	Call GM; lease, trip, agenda
30	Miller contract review
10	ME B-Day
5	Call Jim
20	Set PM (Kit. Mtg.)
35	Call Tom K (Oregon)
30	CK w/WJFK schedule
60	Call TB sales/vm/temp
120	Reactive Time (Misc.)
30	New Training Concept
10	Set JR Lunch

675 min / 60 = 11.25 hrs.

Fig. 2 — Estimating the Time

available, then it does not work, and you need to go back and massage the brain dump and estimated time.

Ask yourself if there is another way to do the activity. Can you do an outline today and then finish the proposal tomorrow when it is due? There will be many days in the beginning that these numbers do not align closely. (For example, if you have 14.5 hours of activities for an eleven-hour day.) If this is the case, see instructions for common mistakes, which are listed later in this chapter. But never move forward without first getting the estimated time to align with the time available in the day.

TIMELINE SETUP

Since most of us are visual thinkers, the timeline helps make your day more visual. This timeline is linear as shown in the example on the following page. When setting this up, follow these simple steps:

1. **Draw a line as noted (or use the TMS notebook template).**

2. **Have a beginning and an end. This represents your day. (Launch at 8:00 a.m. and finish at 5:30 p.m.) Draw a circle at these end points.**

3. **Create the other points based on that specific day's activities (e.g., a 10:00 a.m. to 11:00 a.m. meeting; lunch at noon to 12:30 p.m.).**

4. **Try to keep intervals no more than three hours. If you have a larger gap, try to break it up into two or three parts.**

5. **Now reflect on this diagram. Can you begin to see and feel the structure that makes sense in your day?**

6. **Make the minor adjustments for the right balance. Each day will vary between five to ten blocks of time, which is why each day is unique and needs to be customized rather than using a standard template.**

7. **Now, block out (or color in) the blocks of times where you have a meeting, conference call, or appointment— again to visualize the day.**

8. **Now create a letter (symbol) for each time section (A, B, C, etc.).**

9. **The draft of the timeline is complete.**

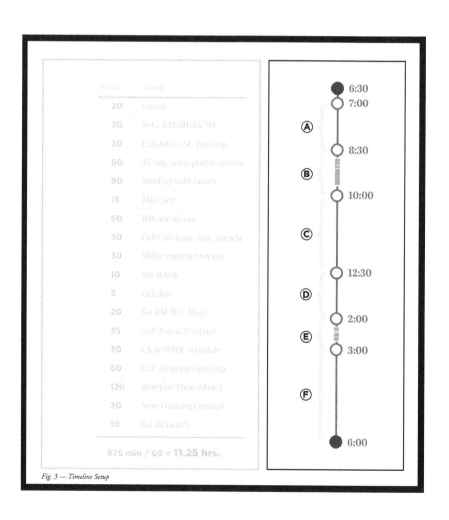

Fig. 3 — Timeline Setup

CONNECT THE BRAIN-DUMP ITEMS TO THE TIMELINE

Now connect the dots between the timeline and the activities list. This step requires thought. Begin with the obvious ones, such as meetings or conference calls. Then think about when in the day you will be in the best frame of mind or have the right urgency to get individual items done. You will have some filler items that can be done anytime—but you need to fit them into the time slot available. This step may sound very simple, but don't rush it. Slow down and think of ways to leverage and multitask to gain valuable minutes.

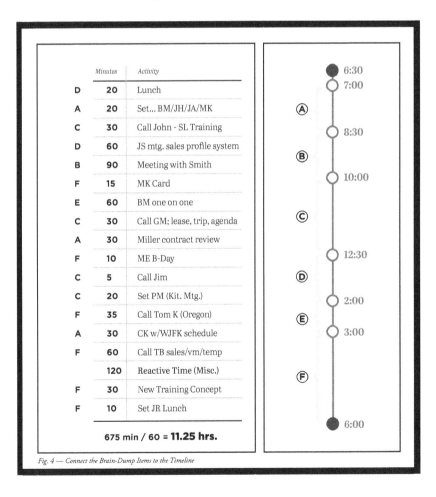

	Minutes	Activity
D	20	Lunch
A	20	Set... BM/JH/JA/MK
C	30	Call John - SL Training
D	60	JS mtg. sales profile system
B	90	Meeting with Smith
F	15	MK Card
E	60	BM one on one
C	30	Call GM; lease, trip, agenda
A	30	Miller contract review
F	10	ME B-Day
C	5	Call Jim
C	20	Set PM (Kit. Mtg.)
F	35	Call Tom K (Oregon)
A	30	CK w/WJFK schedule
F	60	Call TB sales/vm/temp
	120	Reactive Time (Misc.)
F	30	New Training Concept
F	10	Set JR Lunch

675 min / 60 = 11.25 hrs.

Timeline:
- 6:30
- 7:00
- Ⓐ
- 8:30
- Ⓑ
- 10:00
- Ⓒ
- 12:30
- Ⓓ
- 2:00
- Ⓔ
- 3:00
- Ⓕ
- 6:00

Fig. 4 — Connect the Brain-Dump Items to the Timeline

ANALYSIS

Now let's take time to do a simple analysis. Add up all the individual time sections and write them on the left side of the timeline. Then see if they fit the time allowed (e.g., the A = eighty minutes, which fits in a ninety-minute time slot). If they don't (which is common), just move an activity to another time slot or modify the activity's goal so it will fit. Keep in mind that there is some reactive time that will unavoidably slip into time slots, so it is always best to have some wiggle room. *Do not move forward unless everything fits and works.*

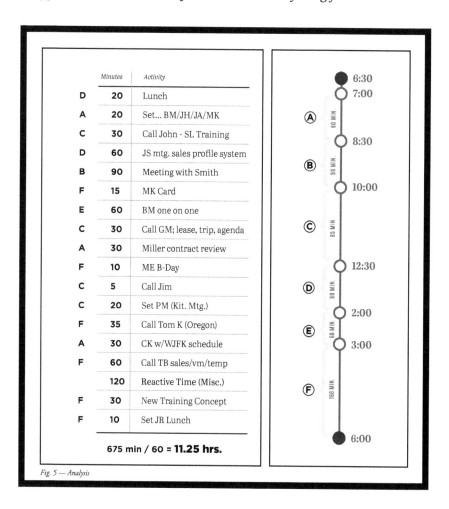

	Minutes	Activity
D	20	Lunch
A	20	Set... BM/JH/JA/MK
C	30	Call John - SL Training
D	60	JS mtg. sales profile system
B	90	Meeting with Smith
F	15	MK Card
E	60	BM one on one
C	30	Call GM; lease, trip, agenda
A	30	Miller contract review
F	10	ME B-Day
C	5	Call Jim
C	20	Set PM (Kit. Mtg.)
F	35	Call Tom K (Oregon)
A	30	CK w/WJFK schedule
F	60	Call TB sales/vm/temp
	120	Reactive Time (Misc.)
F	30	New Training Concept
F	10	Set JR Lunch

675 min / 60 = 11.25 hrs.

Timeline:
- 6:30
- 7:00
- (A) 80 MIN
- 8:30
- (B) 90 MIN
- 10:00
- (C) 85 MIN
- 12:30
- (D) 80 MIN
- 2:00
- (E) 60 MIN
- 3:00
- (F) 160 MIN
- 6:00

Fig. 5 — Analysis

Here are a few important questions to ask yourself before the launch.

The blueprint or road map for your day:

a. Does it work (i.e., do the times fit the activities)?

b. Is this plan aggressive but realistic?

c. Are the activities/pace consistent with your theme and goals for the day?

THE LAUNCH

Congratulations! You now have a blueprint for your day. Take a minute and review it. Try to think about what is missing. Ask yourself, "Is it too aggressive or too conservative?" Before long, you will find the right cadence for you.

Now focus on *only* the A items. Pick any A you want to focus on. And do it! Circle each item as you complete it and then move on to the next one. Think about "aggressive-but-realistic" pace. If you complete all the As and have extra time, grab an item from another time slot and just get it done, or use the little gaps of time to deal

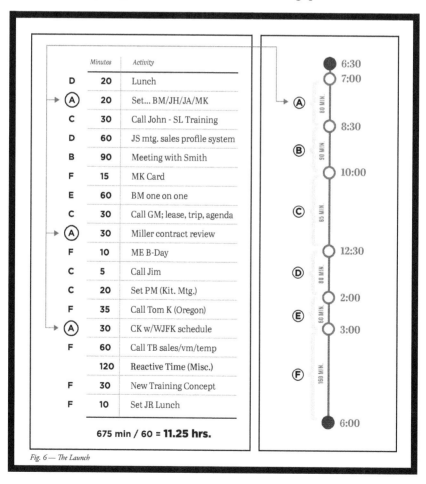

Fig. 6 — The Launch

with reactive things that pop up. You never know exactly when you might slip with some reactive activities later in the day.

MONITORING YOUR PLAN

The most common mistake made with this and other systems is not *monitoring* your plan throughout the day. You will need to monitor it every sixty to ninety minutes. It is easy to make minor adjustments if you know early where you are off or ahead of your plan. This monitoring process will get easier over time. If you get used to carrying the notebook with you, you can do the monitoring in the little gaps of time throughout the day. Use the little gaps of time to monitor.

ADJUSTING YOUR PLAN

While we all hope the day will give you what you planned, unfortunately, it probably will not. You need to build in a process to adjust your game plan. It helps again here to think about football. A good coach does not throw out his game plan after the first ten minutes into the game when he is down by three points. However, at halftime he'll take a serious (and quick) inventory of what's working or not, what the score is, and what the team needs to do in the second half.

Adjusting your time game plan or design is very similar. As you monitor every sixty to ninety minutes, you are making minor tweaks and adjustments. Then, at midday, I encourage you to make a real halftime adjustment. (I generally can do this in a few minutes, so you don't need to make it an event, but in the first thirty days, allow ten minutes for halftime planning.) This halftime adjustment looks at what has been accomplished. It looks at any changes in the goals for the day. It also addresses the things that have popped up and might need to be planned for directly or scheduled for another day.

Again, this planning system is dynamic and a tool that you adjust and manipulate as you go.

I always take a few minutes at the end of each day and review what I accomplished. I look at what requires planning notes or scheduling for future days—and then generally I smile and take a deep breath after having a very successful and productive day.

COMMON MISTAKES PEOPLE MAKE

Lost time is never found again.

BENJAMIN FRANKLIN

Most students of success understand that it can be achieved by being skillful or clever—but also simply by eliminating or avoiding mistakes. For example, when taking a trip, your goal may be to get to your destination safely. If you are driving, you need to avoid accidents and car trouble to arrive safely. So how do you achieve this? You drive defensively by leaving adequate space between cars, you take your car in for regular maintenance, and you avoid potholes or debris in the road. This is a simplistic example, but it also holds true when mastering the TMS. Avoid potential potholes and the likelihood of success increases.

The following are the seven most-common mistakes people make with this TMS.

1. Forcing fourteen hours into a ten-hour day

This is like pouring a quart of milk into a pint jar. It does not work. So why do we attempt this when it comes to our day? Since you are estimating the amount of time things will take, you might be overly optimistic about how long something will take.

It might also be you are overwhelmed and believe if everything miraculously got done, life would be wonderful. Or it could be that you are not allowing or anticipating enough inevitable reactive time in your day. The bottom line is that ninety-five times out of a hundred, you are setting yourself up for failure. It is critical that the time estimated to do your activities is closely aligned with the time allowed for the day, and fourteen hours is

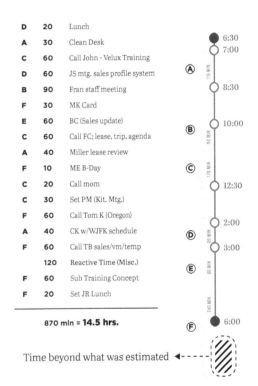

D	20	Lunch
A	30	Clean Desk
C	60	Call John - Velux Training
D	60	JS mtg. sales profile system
B	90	Fran staff meeting
F	30	MK Card
E	60	BC (Sales update)
C	60	Call FC; lease, trip, agenda
A	40	Miller lease review
F	10	ME B-Day
C	20	Call mom
C	30	Set PM (Kit. Mtg.)
F	60	Call Tom K (Oregon)
A	40	CK w/WJFK schedule
F	60	Call TB sales/vm/temp
	120	Reactive Time (Misc.)
F	60	Sub Training Concept
F	20	Set JR Lunch

870 min = 14.5 hrs.

Time beyond what was estimated ◀- - - -

not even close! As illustrated here, you need to go back and work your brain-dump activities. Ask if there are other ways to communicate or accomplish the task in a shorter amount of time. I prefer not to push things completely to the next day. You may want to break an item down so you can at least inch it forward today, then complete it on a future day.

2. Doing your TMS planning in the wrong place/time

Here's a simple checklist to successful planning. If the answer to any of these is no, then fix it, or you will likely fail.

a. **Is it quiet enough for you to concentrate?** (Not at the breakfast table with the kids or in a place you get interrupted, like a crowded office.)

b. **Do you have enough time (a minimum of thirty minutes) to properly plan?** If you only have fifteen minutes, it is a rough sketch of your day—not a plan.

c. **Is it in the morning—not the evening before?** (Some things happen overnight that can make your design flawed.)

3. Not monitoring

This is a journey that requires a map to help you navigate successfully. By reviewing your design every sixty to ninety minutes, you are making sure you don't miss an exit. If you have a detour in your journey (and you will), you can make minor adjustments to reach your destination or goal. Always carry your notebook with you so you can use the little gaps of time to monitor your progress.

4. Allowing for too many interruptions

While you don't want to be rude or disrespectful, it is essential that you treat yourself with the same level of importance and reverence that you treat others. When someone interrupts you, consider asking if you can address his or her issue on your schedule rather than immediately dropping everything. This is a well-planned journey, and if you are constantly interrupted, you will never reach your destination on time. Go back to the reactive versus proactive chapter and try to improve with the techniques.

5. Brain-dump items are too general

There is an important balance for your brain-dump items. You don't want them to be too detailed (e.g., "fill my coffee cup"), but the more common mistake is making them too broad. Consider breaking a larger item into several smaller parts. For example, listing "Work on the Jones project" would be too broad to accurately estimate the time required. A better approach is to break the larger item into several smaller tasks:

 a. Jones outline *(twenty minutes)*

 b. Jones rough draft *(forty minutes)*

 c. Get feedback on draft from Mary *(twenty minutes)*

By breaking an item into parts, you will be able to better estimate the time required. You also may be able to accomplish some parts at different times of the day rather than in one sitting.

6. Getting too creative

I am a creative person, but you don't need to be to make the TMS work for you. A common mistake is that creative people want to modify or tweak my system. They like to cross things out rather than circle the letters. They try to be efficient by developing a template for the design that can save them time. They do the techniques at night versus in the morning. I can go on and on, but the message is this: for the first thirty days follow these techniques. 100 percent! When people struggle or fall off the wagon, it is generally because they veer off the road by getting too creative.

7. Giving up too soon

The first week is tough for everyone. You are changing your basic daily patterns. You are using muscles that you may not be used to using. Before beginning this process, you still filled your day with something that took thirty or forty minutes, and now you are adding to an already busy schedule. The reason I ask for a thirty-day commitment is that, like any other habit, it takes twenty to thirty days to establish the behavior. I also know you will feel much better and begin to accomplish the "why" goals. Once you experience some control over your day and see the ROI, you will continue to be vested into the system. Don't give up too soon!

This system does not require an advanced degree or a high level of skill or intelligence. It does require the right mind-set, a little time, and the diligence to stick to it.

THE TOP-TEN TMS QUESTIONS ANSWERED

1. Do I need to do this planning process over the weekend?

No. I find most people have a very different rhythm or cadence over the weekend. Some like to surrender control to their family or their personal life, or just go with the flow and let the day control them. Others just need to recharge. For those who need a more structured plan over the weekend, this planning process (or a slight variation of it) still works. Again, this is a personal planning tool to help you feel better and more fulfilled, not a process to be obsessed with.

2. Can I use another type of notebook (a smaller or a fancy binder)?

No. The 8.5" x 11" size is important. You need to be able to see the entire day to massage and work it. You need space to feel like you have room to add notes (which you can refer to the next day). By using a spiral notebook, you will not lose pages, and you can easily refer to a phone number or a note to yourself several days or weeks later. The scale and type of the notebook does matter.

3. Can I do this planning process the night before when I have an early meeting the next day?

No, sorry. I recommend getting up thirty minutes earlier to do the process, or wait until after that early meeting to design the rest of the day. I have had many people try doing it the night before, and the results have not been good. Just like when traveling, the weather changes and flights get delayed. You need to do this process in real time. If you have a lot whirling in your head the night before, then just make a mini to-do list that you can use in your planning process the next morning.

4. Should I prioritize my brain dump?

Not really. I am a big believer that your brain dump needs to be a "stream-of-consciousness" process. Let the day flow out. Jot down the items as fast as they flow out of your head. After you have everything out and have reviewed your calendar, other tools, notes, etc., then you can manipulate the items and activities to determine whether you want to accomplish them today or not. You also can ask yourself, "When is the best time to accomplish the activities?" I find some of the pressing priorities are like black clouds above you, so you might want to address them early to get the sun to shine in the afternoon.

5. What if I am not sure when I should do an item?

This is not a problem. You can always pick two time slots for an item (i.e., B and E). You still need to estimate the time involved the same way. Then you can do it in the time slot that works best in the moment. If you have a list of several minor things, you can also use X, which is time-slot neutral, and then knock these minor items off when you have a few minutes between things.

6. What if my brain-dump activities only add up to six hours of time in a ten-hour day?

Although this is rare for me (and most busy people), I generally begin to focus on and stretch my medium- and longer-term muscles. I ask myself if I can move something forward from a future day. I look at my long-term goals and try to inch something forward. I also try to weave more personal interests in when they occur (like a lunch with my daughter or calls to some old friends). Again, it is important to create a plan that fills the day properly (including reactive time), and then work the plan. That is where the fulfillment comes. So find those additional items to fill the day. You will feel better and more fulfilled.

7. Can I make changes in the plan during the day?

Yes. You must. You might have an appointment that moves or someone shows up late. You also might need to get in touch with someone you thought you could reach in the morning but were not able to. As discussed, the monitoring and tweaking of the plan is as important as the plan itself. You might make three to seven minor changes and maybe even one or two major changes in the design during the day. Again, this is like a football game. If the score is where you want it to be after the first quarter, then stick to the original plan. If the score is off by a lot, then you adjust your plan. If at halftime, you are down twenty to zero, you need a new game plan for the second half. The dynamic is the same with your day. Monitor and then decide to stick to the plan or adjust it as needed.

8. How do I weave in a plan for reading and responding to the copious amount of e-mails I get daily?

The number of e-mails you get can vary quite a bit. I find when I travel, I get 50 percent of the e-mails that I do when I am in my office. I also find that certain days of the week I get more than others. I have surveyed many professional people, and the number of e-mails they receive daily varies from thirty-five to three hundred. The reason I set this in context is that I believe you need to take better control over your e-mails. For example, I did an experiment for a week. As a proactive, friendly guy, I tended to respond to e-mails even when I was not asked to. I decided to try not responding unless asked—and my e-mails dropped by 40 percent. Interesting! Now I have found a balance. Another technique I use is to draft an e-mail then save it and respond later that day in a more thoughtful or careful way (we all know that e-mail responses can be tricky). To go back to the question, if I have several important e-mails to respond to, I would carve out a time (even if only fifteen minutes) to do it. Otherwise, most people can fit them into the reactive time slots available.

9. How close does the time for my brain-dump list need to be to the total amount of time available for the day?

My general rule is to not begin the day if there is a thirty-minute or more variance. If you have eleven and a half hours of activities in your brain dump and only ten hours available in your day, then you need to work it more. First go back and make sure you were not too liberal with your time. Then ask if there are better or more effective ways to do some items. Consider shortening a meeting from sixty to fifty minutes. Break a project into parts and move one part into another day (e.g., do a draft today, then the final tomorrow). Is there a different way to accomplish some of the items on your list? Send an e-mail to someone instead of making a more time-consuming phone call. While tweaking will take some time, you want to set yourself up to succeed. So, yes, the plan needs to come very close to the amount of time available in your day.

10. What if my day crashes and burns?

Hopefully this will only happen occasionally. It usually is a product of a major fire or just letting it get out of control. The real question is, "How did you feel at the end of the day?" Not great, right? So by being more disciplined and by monitoring more carefully, you will increase the odds of a great day. Before they begin to utilize this system, most people only have one or two good days per week. After using this system, you will increase that to three or four great days per week. If the nature of your work is more firefighting or reactionary, you will have a tough time staying on track. It's important to remember, this is all about improvement, not perfection. So, when this happens, just make sure the next day does not blow up on you too.

TIME MASTERY IN ACTION

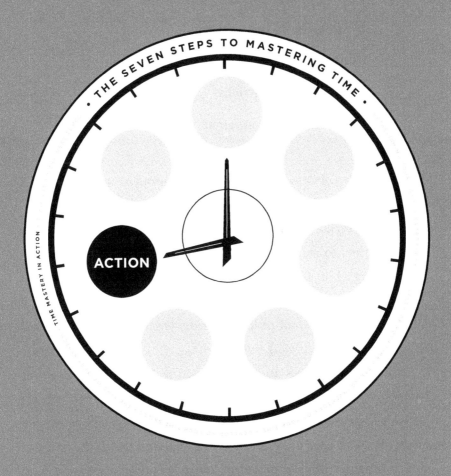

You can't stop time. You can't capture light. You can only turn your face up and let it rain down.

KIM EDWARDS

Mastering anything you put your mind to can be the difference between being good and being great. Years ago, I read about the four stages to mastery as "baby steps to success." While these steps need to be made relevant to anything you want to master, it does help you to see mastery as a process or a journey.

The four stages to mastery:

1. **Unconsciously incompetent**

2. **Consciously incompetent**

3. **Consciously competent**

4. **Unconsciously competent**

The best way to understand this concept is through a simple example familiar to most of us: learning to ride a bike.

When you are three years old, you are *unconsciously incompetent* when it comes to riding a bike. At that age, most have not thought about riding a bike or even experimented.

At six or seven, you get you your first bike. You get on it and fall. While you strongly want to learn to ride, you don't yet think it will happen. You are *consciously incompetent.*

After some scrapes and bruises, you finally begin to get your balance. You are actually riding. You may not ride well, but you are entering stage three of mastery (*consciously competent*). While you are happy that you have accomplished this, you find it stressful and not a very relaxing riding experience. You're spending a lot of mental energy just trying not to fall off the bike.

After many hours of riding and practice you begin to move into stage four of mastery, when you become *unconsciously competent.* You don't have to think about being able to ride. You now can experiment with some riding tricks. You now begin to enjoy the view. You now can have a comfortable conversation with someone riding with you. All these are early stage-four mastery experiences. Now you really begin to see the return on the investment of learning and mastering bike riding.

I share this simple analogy because it is parallel to the higher levels of time mastery. If you want to see the maximum returns in time mastery you need to become a student of success. You need to become so proficient at the system and the subject that you become *unconsciously competent* at planning your day. When you reach this level, you not only automatically and gracefully use the system, but you can go much deeper and find answers to questions and ways to be more effective.

As much as I would like to give you a magic pill to get there, it really just takes three things:

> **Commitment:** If you lose the commitment to master time you will fall off the wagon and fail.
>
> **Focus:** You need to stay laser-focused on improving your skills every day.
>
> **Capital:** It requires an investment of time to gain time mastery.

Generally, after about thirty days, you can reach level three of mastery, but level four is a continuous improvement process. The reason you want to push, however, is so you can continue to gain time-mastery insights and benefit (ROI) year after year. People who reach the fourth level of mastery gain hundreds of hours a year of more effective time. They are less stressed, and they accomplish more. They keep promises and exceed expectations. Overall they feel better and more fulfilled.

Try to think in terms of baby steps. Be patient with yourself. Don't forget to celebrate the progress as you continue to find the energy and discipline to get there.

TIME MYTHS

I need to wear a watch. This is not true if it is for telling the time. Many years ago, my wife bought me a new watch. After about five years, the band broke. I took it to the jeweler, who said the cost to fix the band was as much as the watch itself. So I did not get it fixed and stopped wearing a watch until I could replace it. At first I was uncomfortable not always being able to check the time. I thought I would run late. But after a month or so, I had trained my brain to be sensitive to the time and could predict it very accurately. This is a skill/muscle, not magic. This is all about being in the moment and being in touch with time. When I am in a meeting or on a conference call, my body tells me when I am getting close to sixty minutes or when it is about 1:00 p.m. Again, it sounds a little mystical, but I know others who have also developed these skills.

MASTERY TIPS

A famous architect (Mies van der Rohe) said, "God is in the details." This is definitely true when it comes to mastering time. After you have the blocking and tackling down in the system, then there are some tips that increase the effectiveness and where you can see increased returns.

The following are my top-ten tips to master the TMS:

1. Ask great questions during the planning process.

And know the important answers on a subconscious level.

    a.   Why am I doing this?

    b.   Is there another way to accomplish it?

    c.   How can I leverage this or expand the return?

By simply asking, you will find the plan will be more meaningful. You will find five or ten minutes here and there that add up to thirty to sixty minutes of dividend in the day.

2. Fill the page.

This system is designed to be done on an 8.5" x 11" notebook because that should represent a full day's worth of brain-dump activities (see examples). If your brain dump is only filling half of the page, go deeper. Add smaller items (a call or a few notes) that, when accomplished, can make a difference between a good day and a great one.

3. Confirm.

I like to send out quick confirmations in the morning in the first time slot (or before) regarding the meetings or calls that I am planning on. It is good to confirm what you expect. Otherwise your day gets thrown off by people forgetting, canceling, or running late

4. Use X when you are not sure.

As you are hooking the timeline into the brain-dump items, you want to match a letter with the time slot. However, these are filler items that really could be done in just about any time slot. I recommend using X. Then as you are moving through your day, either lock these in at particular slots—or just knock them out as you see fit. The win is getting it done, not fitting it into the correct time slot.

5. Bounce around.

After you have the basic process down (where you are consciously competent), you might find there are benefits on some days to bouncing the order of the steps around a little. For example, if I am feeling like the day is crammed, I might go ahead and begin a rough timeline so I can visualize my day before I get too deep into my brain dump. I might also go to the other tools that are highlighted in the "taking it to the next level" chapter, like the stress cloud,[1] which may influence what I want my activities to be that day or how aggressive I want to be. Over time you will find this process is very meditative, so you might wander a bit, as long as you end up with an end plan for the day.

---

1   *See explanation on page 136.*

6. Leverage the gaps.

Often what makes a day great is the little things you accomplish, not just the big to-do items. As you are analyzing the rough design (before launch), try to focus on the gaps. The gaps are the time between things. It could be fifteen minutes between meetings or calls, or it could be the time to drive twenty minutes to get to an appointment. I generally will hit five to fifteen small actions/add-ons a day in these gaps. But the key is to plan them. You may want to give some of these an X time slot, if you have multiple gaps.

7. Master world-class voicemails.

I know voicemails can be annoying and frustrating, but they are an excellent time-mastery tool if done well. When you are doing your morning planning, ask yourself if a voicemail may be an efficient way to communicate. If the answer is yes, then plan for it. If you want to leave a voicemail, the best time to do it is when you know the other person won't be answering the call (a time of day while they are in a meeting or at the gym). Jot down a little outline of what you want to communicate. Make the message concise, but complete enough. Then send a text or e-mail saying you left a "lengthy" voicemail and ask for a reply. You can save twenty to thirty minutes a day by doing this sort of world-class voicemailing. And that can add up to sixty hours a year. This does take a little practice and preparation, but the key is to begin to plan them, not just react when the other person does not answer his or her phone.

8. Multitask.

Our ability to multitask today is greater than ever. The speed at which our brains must process is faster. Our ability to do two or three things at once competently is better. It is critical that you are uber-focused when you need to be, but you can also plan to do more than one thing during some activities. Again, once you have mastered the basic planning system, then ask yourself during the morning planning session if they are activities that can be done while doing something else. These, by the way, may be personal, too. For example, you can clean up e-mails when on a group conference call, or you can sit outside and get fresh air to recharge during a call, or you can walk your dog and talk on the phone.

9. Invest in the tools.

There are many simple technology tools that can make things easier. Here are a few I use:

a. Using a wireless headset for calls allows me to move about and do other simple tasks while on calls. This saves me twenty minutes a day, which equals sixty hours a year.

b. I use a phone camera to text/e-mail images.

c. The voice recorder on the phone allows me to record text/e-mail messages. I find these little recordings are a great way to communicate effectively. Then I blast them out to the recipient(s).

d. Get yourself a high-quality day timer. It must have extra pages for your additional planning tools and a pocket in the back for goal-tracking tools and other important information. I religiously carry one of these around all the time, so I chose one that looks presentable when I pull it out. I find this to be an important tool for planning.

10. Set up a mobile office.

While safe driving is always the top priority, you can also leverage your time in the car. Here are three ways to use/think of your mobile office:

1. **It's a communication command center.** Make sure you have all the tools, both high tech and high touch.

2. **It's a mobile university.** This is a great training opportunity; listen to podcasts, training CDs, books, etc.

3. **It's a think tank.** Use this time for deeper reflection on important things that require some meditativeness. Make a list of questions you want to ask yourself while driving.

If you know you are going to be in your car for commuting or for chunks of time during the day or week, then really make it a priority to plan in these gaps of times. Doing this also gives you greater freedom when you know the office is mobile and you can accomplish many things on the move.

TIME MYTHS

An appointment means it's going to happen. An appointment is just a placeholder until it is confirmed. Think how many times appointments have been postponed or cancelled. Then just multiply the amount of time this would waste. It represents hundreds of hours in a year. If you can be disciplined about not assuming a meeting or appointment is going to happen unless you confirm it, you will increase your effectiveness substantially. Adding this proactivity to your thinking will save time and make you more effective.

TAKING IT TO THE NEXT LEVEL

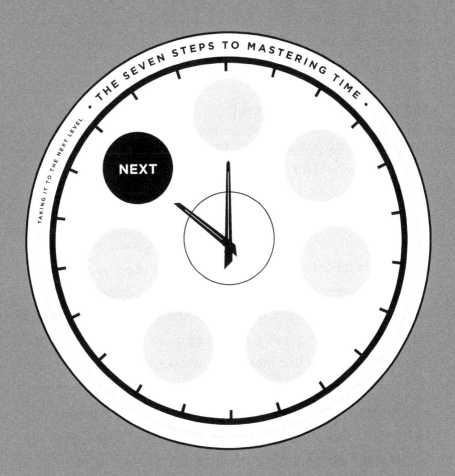

Practice makes perfect.

UNKNOWN

After you have gotten to stage three of mastery and you are beginning to enter stage four (*unconsciously competent*), you can begin to weave in other planning tools and techniques to increase your mastery of time and your success. Some of these "taking it to the next level" tools have been developed to look at time from a different angle and in different intervals. While you will be able to benefit from these, I also encourage you to now begin to get a little more creative and use this methodology to customize and develop your own tools. While I continue to be a very low-tech person, I recognize that by leveraging technology you may also gain a few insights and efficiency in your day.

ANNUAL/QUARTERLY PLANNING

One tool I developed and use is a tool for medium- or longer-term planning. I call it the T-9 (Top 9) tool.

The idea of this tool comes from my annual planning process. At the end of every year I take two or three days to plan the following year. (You don't have to wait until the end of the year to do this.) This is sort of like hibernating for three days and is a personal/professional strategic-planning process. I generally begin by doing a deep-dive inventory. This is where I think about and reflect on the previous year. I try to drill into hard data and metrics as well as feelings and emotions. I try to solicit input from my personal and professional circles of influence. Over the years I have found that the best way to take this inventory is in specific categories rather than in one big bite. I have found that nine to ten categories work best to yield goals and actions that I can monitor effectively.

The categories I use are:

1. My health (physical/mental/emotional)

2. My wife

3. My family

4. My friends/relationships

5. My home

6. My financials

7. My fun/fulfillment

8. My work

9. My community

You can certainly add or delete from this list, but I find nine a good number of categories. For a visualization of the T-9 tool, see page 132.

The process:

1. Think about a few overriding themes for the year that touch most of the categories. These can be a product of where you are now, something you want to change, or something you want to continue doing. These themes are the glue that touches most of the categories. Some of my themes for the year I wrote this book (2017):

    a. Balance

    b. Time is the key

    c. Be thirsty

    d. Good health = +++

    e. Avoid mistakes

    f. Say no, too

THE T-9 TOOL

ANNUAL THEMES	Balance • Time Is the Key • Be Thirsty		
Themes	1st Quarter	2nd Quarter	Annual Goals
Health Age Well / Be Active / Gain Knowledge	Lose five pounds by cutting back on dessert/drinking / Doctor's appt.		Weight to 185 lbs. / Bike to beach / Develop a new hobby
Wife			
Family			
Relationships			
Home			
Financials			
Fulfillment			
Professional Stay relevant / 20% fresh / Authority	Book manuscript 90% / Invest more time in Harvard		Write two books / Create Remodeling-Mastery Boot Camp
Community			

2. Then for each subcategory have some subthemes:

    a. Health category themes:

        i. Age well

        ii. Be active

        iii. Gain knowledge

    b. For the professional category:

        i. Stay relevant

        ii. 20% fresh

        iii. Authority

While I think these themes are important, they just need to give direction. They are not the actions or necessarily the goal.

3. The next steps are to establish the actions for each. Begin with some annual goals for each category. For example:

    a. Health:

        i. Weight to 185 lbs.

        ii. Bike to beach

        iii. Develop a new hobby

    b. Professional:

        i. Write two books

        ii. Create Remodeling-Mastery Boot Camp

        iii. Write one more monthly column/blog

4. With these overarching themes and the individual subthemes in mind, try to come up with three to five actions in the first quarter for each. For example, for the

category of health and the previous themes (age well / be active / gain knowledge), the first quarter actions are:

a.   Lose five pounds by cutting back on dessert/drinking.

b.   Avg. 4 x week of 30 to 60 min. of exercise.

c.   Dr. apt for a check up.

d.   Travel well (pack to eat / exercise).

e.   Get a DNA test.

For the professional category:

a.   Book manuscript 90%.

b.   Avg. 40 hours per week with clients.

c.   Deeper magazine relationship.

d.   Invest more time in Harvard.

e.   Move Thought-Leaders program forward.

I generally prefer to have a detailed next quarter and a loose following quarter (it gets readjusted on a monthly basis).

After you have this road map, you need a system to monitor it. I generally like to do a sixty- to ninety-minute-deep daily plan every Monday. In this additional time, I review the top-nine areas of my life, or my T-9 (and the other following tools). I ask myself how I can move these actions in my day and week. I reflect on the themes to make sure I continue to have my priorities right.

You can really take it to the next level with this simple tool.

GOAL-SETTING TOOL

A goal without a plan is just a wish.

ANTOINE DE SAINT-EXUPÉRY

There are many goal-setting tools that you can use, but I have learned over the years that none will work unless it is:

1. **Meaningful.** Really thought through both in importance and realistic timing.

2. **Concise.** I have had short ones and long ones, but the ones I can review and think about easily are the best. By the way, you may have mountains of back-up data/thoughts/ notes, but what you look at regularly needs to be concise (ideally one page).

3. **In bite-size pieces.** You can't eat a pizza in one bite. By breaking goals into parts both in categories and in time frames, you can think through and really focus

So, with all that said, I like to begin with a simple spreadsheet or list using my T 9 categories.

I then like to list a few long-term (three- to five-year) goals for each. It is important that you take into account how time changes for other people involved (e.g., if one of the goals is that you want to take your kids on a cross-country trip, then keep in mind that—if they are ten and twelve years old now—in five years they will be fifteen and seventeen and may not be interested in going on the trip with you).

I encourage you to list the stretch goals. Try to also write down the obstacles or potholes that would keep you from reaching this goal (like money, time, health etc.).

Then I try to narrow this down to three big goals from each category.

Next you want to move from five years, down to three, then down to the coming year.

Generally, this will result in just a few big goals for the year. I like to create a one-page chart with each of these goals. I can read on a weekly basis and ask myself: How can I inch this goal along this week? When should I lock this event or goal into my calendar (based on my other activities)? Is this goal still relevant and aggressive but realistic?

STRESS CLOUDS

As you know by now, I am a visual thinker. I can communicate with words; however, if I can find a metaphor or a diagram to express a concept or an idea, then my level of mastery on the subject increases exponentially. I only began using this technique or tool a few years before this writing, but it has made a big difference in my ability to balance, control, and reduce my stress. Unlike some of the other tools, I only pull this one out when I need it (when I am feeling some overwhelm and stress). It is sort of like taking an aspirin when you have a headache.

The metaphor is what I call "stress clouds." On a bright, sunny day, there are no clouds in the sky versus a dark, dreary day when the cloud cover is so thick that you cannot see the sun at all. Needless to say, most days are in between, with a few clouds. Being a sun guy (as most people are) I feel better and more energized on the sunny days versus feeling sad and a little depressed on the no-sun days.

In your day or week, we all have stress clouds. Most can handle several small ones and still feel good. Some can handle one big one as long as there are not any little ones creeping in.

The purpose of this tool/exercise is to identify what these clouds are, how big they are, and what is needed to make them go away or vaporize.

The first step I take is to draw myself as a simple stick figure.

CLEAR SKIES

Then I begin to draw the clouds. The sizes or shapes vary depending on the level of stress that they are causing me. For example, if I have a big speaking presentation on a new topic in four days and I am not feeling like I have nailed it, I may draw a big cloud and write the name of the talk in it. If, on the other hand, I have the same presentation and I feel fully prepared but need to confirm a few details to finalize it, I will draw a little cloud.

Now, sticking to the metaphor, the big cloud blocks the sun more than the little one. I continue to create different clouds from different places (personal, health, relationship strain, and other projects to complete). What might be adding to the stress that I am feeling?

Then I take a couple of minutes to look at the visual holistically. I ask myself, does this represent the stress that I am feeling? How would I feel if some of this stress were gone? Do I believe I can reduce these stress clouds? Is there someone else who can help me with this?

Then I write out two to five actions steps on a notebook page for each cloud that would shrink or vaporize the cloud.

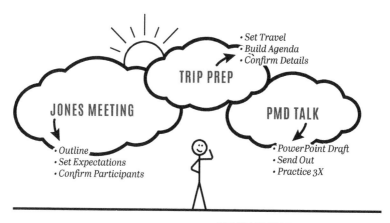

Then I keep this piece of paper with me as I am doing my daily planning. Generally, I cannot attack all the items on that day, or even in a couple of days, but I always feel better knowing that I am in control, and I recognize the stress is usually something that can be reduced quickly, if I take action.

IN CLOSING

Unexpressed good thoughts aren't worth squat!

KEN BLANCHARD

O ver the last twenty-five years, I have made huge strides in mastering my time. These are strides, not final destinations. These strides have given me real and meaningful returns. By sharing these insights and the time-management system, I hope you will be able to see the same returns in months, not years.

As I shared earlier in this book, the goal is to first focus on strong "whys," and they will give you the conviction to stick with the system.

The following are what you should expect to achieve:

- Reduce stress. (This may be the biggest benefit for many people.)

- Accomplish more.

- Stay on track with your goals and resolutions.

- Think more clearly.

- Look longer term.

- Keep important promises.

- Exceed expectations.

- Be more predictable.

- Have time for other priorities.

- Have control of your destiny.

How each person processes this material is very personal. Some of you may have found it interesting and will tuck away a nugget or two to use when it is relevant to you. Others will be back to your old habits and continue to feel the stress of having others control your day. (I hope when the pain is great enough you will remember to dust this off and revisit the advice I have shared.) Then there will be a handful of the students of success. You are the ones who embrace change, shift your thinking, and develop the habits to achieve the results.

Having taught these time-mastery techniques to thousands of people, I am not here to judge which group you fall into. I want you to be aware that being in control of your day is a *choice*. If you choose to take control, then this summary is just the beginning. The following are some further tips as you dive into this process.

1. It takes time to develop new habits, so be patient with yourself.

2. We all need a coach, so grab a friend or reach out to me if you need help.

3. Visualize and believe in the rewards of mastering time.

4. If you fail to plan, then plan to fail.

5. Tell others about your thirst to improve, and they will be your cheerleaders for success

This book is only one piece of the time-mastery jigsaw puzzle. It may be the centerpiece, but you should think about adding some of these other tools to be successful:

1. Contact Mark G. Richardson for relavant links and access to the below.

2. Watch the time-mastery video to see the actual techniques being done.

3. Listen to the time-mastery audio, where I will walk you through these techniques and concepts.

4. Check out the time-mastery webinar (a sixty-minute webinar to supplement your learning).

5. Sign up for a time-mastery workshop (see the site for dates).

6. Seek out one-on-one time coaching.

7. Call the time-mastery "hotline."

Thank you. I wish you well in your journey to take control of your day and master your time!

ABOUT THE AUTHOR

MARK G. RICHARDSON's involvement in construction, design, and business spans more than three decades. A graduate of the School of Architecture at Virginia Tech, his career has been defined by leadership and an entrepreneurial spirit. As the former Co-Chairman and President of Case, he led the growth of over 1,000 percent by expanding services and market reach. For ten years he hosted "At Home with Mark Richardson," a weekly radio show dedicated to bringing a slice of the remodeling industry to consumers and practitioners alike. Mark's passion for teaching and speaking generally takes complex ideas and simplifies things for diverse groups.

Mark is a guest lecturer for MBA programs at Virginia Tech, Georgetown University, Maryland University, and George Washington University. He serves as a business advisor to many business sectors from small practices to major corporations. In 2007 he developed a series of online business workshops and videos designed to offer professional, effective, and intelligent business practices from business fitness to sales and marketing strategies.

Mark is a Sr. Fellow at Harvard University's Joint Center for Housing Studies and sits on many boards including Systems Pavers, N. Kelly Companies, Harrell, BBB, Revere Bank, and Advantage Media Group. He is also a regular columnist for *Professional Remodeler, Professional Builder,* and *Big Growers* magazines. Other Mark Richardson vehicles include: The Remodeling Thirty Day Fitness Program, Remodeling Live, and Business over Breakfast series. In 2006 Mark was named Entrepreneur of the Year with Ernst and Young. In 2008 Mark was inducted into the National Association of Home Builders Hall of Fame.

Mark continues to write, speak, and consult with diverse organizations in an effort to help them improve and grow. He can be reached at mrichardson@mgrichardson.com.

"A GIFT OF TIME"

Time Mastery Workbook

Mark G. Richardson

mrichardson@mgrichardson.com

Printed in the USA
CPSIA information can be obtained
at www.ICGtesting.com
JSHW012053140824
68134JS00035B/3419